Antique Glass
and Glass Collecting

Antique Glass
and Glass Collecting

Frank Davis

Hamlyn

London · New York · Sydney · Toronto

Published by
The Hamlyn Publishing Group Limited
London · New York · Sydney · Toronto
Hamlyn House, Feltham, Middlesex, England

© copyright The Hamlyn Publishing Group Limited 1973

ISBN 0 600 33909 2

Printed by
Sir Joseph Causton & Sons Ltd
London and Eastleigh

Endpapers. **The interior of a typical glass-house of the eighteenth century. From Diderot's Encyclopedia, Vol. X.**
Title Page
1 Syrian enamelled mosque lamp bearing the name of the Mameluke Sultan of Egypt, Baybars II (1309–10). Victoria and Albert Museum, London.

2 'The Luck of Edenhall'. Syrian, thirteenth to fourteenth century. Victoria and Albert Museum, London.

Contents

Early Days

3 The mask of Tutankhamun. Solid gold beaten and burnished. The stripes of the headdress are of blue glass paste imitating lapis lazuli, *c.* 1352 BC. The Egyptian Museum, Cairo.

Numbers in the margins refer to illustrations mentioned in the text

No doubt if one really wanted to speak with authority about glass one would spend six months keeping one's eyes open in a modern glass factory and five years travelling about Europe and America seeing everything there is to be seen in public and private collections. Very few of us have either money or time to spare for such delectable self-indulgence and so we have to make do with what is available in museums, among the few (and I must add very knowledgeable) dealers and with the often distinguished, sometimes trivial, collections which appear from time to time in the auction rooms.

Museums are immensely important to the newcomer, for their glasses are normally logically and ingeniously displayed and – certainly in the case of the Victoria and Albert Museum – cover a very wide field. There is no other place in England, for instance, where one can see such a splendid array of Spanish glass; apart from this collection most of us would be unaware that glass with a specially Spanish flavour had ever been made.

Perhaps newcomers, faced at first by such marvels from so many countries, will take some time to get their bearings, but a little patience, a refusal to see too many objects in one afternoon and a determination not to wander off along side tracks will soon enable them to sort things out into a distinct pattern. Before long they will become fascinated by this magical material and by the slow process, experiment after experiment during many centuries, which resulted in so many masterpieces.

The first question to be answered is 'What is Glass?' It is an artificial substance 'produced by the fusion of silica in the form of sand, flint or quartz, in a furnace, with the aid of an alkaline flux, which may be either potash or soda'. The resultant material is known to glass-makers as 'the metal'. This definition is correct, it describes the essentials, but for practical purposes in order to make a useful, long-lasting glass, small quantities of other substances must be added – limestone sometimes or chalk or oxide of lead – this last particularly in England.

We take glass so much for granted in our world of today that we are liable to forget what a remarkable substance it is. When viscous, it can be blown and moulded into ingenious, often noble shapes, it can be coloured throughout, it can be decorated with gilding and enamelled, it reflects light, it is normally, though not invariably, translucent, it can add splendour and sparkle to any room and it is, of course, though that side of its usefulness is beyond the scope of this book, invaluable in industry.

Once upon a time – so the story goes, and all worthwhile fairy-tales should begin in this way – Phœnician merchants returning from Egypt with, among other goods, a cargo of natron (a natural carbonate of soda) hauled up their ship on the sand at the mouth of the river Belus and rested their cooking-pots upon lumps of natron. They found, when their fire had died down, that the natron had combined with the sand to form glass; thus did a great industry come into being. The story is romantic nonsense, for glass was made in Egypt centuries earlier. All we can say is that the sand by the Belus was used by the glass-workers of Sidon to manufacture their glass vessels, which were famous in the Roman world, and the story was surely put about to explain Sidon's pre-eminence as a glass-making centre.

The prior claims of Egypt to the discovery seem established firmly enough, for stone beads have been found which are covered with a glass glaze and which can be dated to about 4000 BC. The discovery may well have been due to chance – great technical advances often are – but it was many centuries before vessels of glass were made. At first they were formed by, as it were, wrapping the viscous metal round a core of clay and then, when the glass was cold, removing the core. This was the method, plus moulding and polishing, in use from about the fifteenth century BC onwards until, at the beginning of our era, some unknown glass-maker, almost certainly in Syria, found that it was possible to dip a hollow iron tube into a hot mass of glass and, by blowing through the other end of the tube, fashion the viscous mass into various shapes – a discovery which, in its effect upon glass manufacture, was as revolutionary as the discovery of the internal combustion engine. There was no basic technical change in the industry for nearly two thousand years when modern methods of manufacture, pressing the metals in moulds, for instance, were introduced.

Of the essential ingredients necessary for glass-making, the most easily obtainable was naturally sand, the purer the better. The Venetians used the white pebbles taken from the Ticino, and in England our experimenters began to use powdered flints. The essential alkali presented a more difficult problem. The Egyptians probably used natron at first, for large deposits lay ready to hand, but in time this very impure material was replaced throughout the Mediterranean world by the ash of various sea plants. By the fifteenth century most of this sea-plant-ash, known in all glass-making centres as *barilla,* was derived from Southern Spain and was highly esteemed.

Inland, and for ordinary coarse glass, glassmen burnt bracken and beech from the forests and the potash derived from that served well enough – hence the term *Waldglas* in Germany, *verre de fougère* in France and *forest glass* in England. English, German and Bohemian glass was usually made with potash, the glass of other countries, notably Venetian, with soda. Today both substances are used in the production of commercial glass.

So much for the broad outline. But as time passed it was found that lime could be a useful ingredient, and from the late seventeenth century the German-speaking lands (Bohemia and Silesia) were able to develop their admirable crystal glass by the addition of chalk, which is carbonate

4 Two-handled bowl. Roman, first century AD. A type more common in silver. Victoria and Albert Museum, London.

22, 29 of lime. During this same half century England, thanks to the inventiveness of George Ravenscroft, found that the addition of as much, sometimes, as 25 per cent of lead by weight, resulted in a metal remarkable for brilliancy and for its power to disperse light. We have reason to boast about the quality of this English 'glass-of-lead' while at the same time recognising that we found no imitators – others preferred their own well-tried methods. What German and English makers did accomplish was to break the monopoly which Venice had held since the Middle Ages.

The natural quartz which we know as rock-crystal had always been admired and glassmen spent generations getting as near to its basic, colourless purity as they could – and in due course succeeded. But meanwhile, during many centuries, they were no less fascinated by the possibilities of colour. I am not speaking for the moment of enamel colours painted on after the glass had been made, but of colouring matter introduced into the material ('the batch') before it went into the furnace, so that the finished vessel was coloured through and through.

One obvious use for coloured glass was to substitute it for genuine precious stones; the practice was not at all uncommon when a reliquary or a cup was required for a church. There was nothing reprehensible in this. People were extremely vague and the boundary between the authentic and the copy was by no means a fixture, for were not alchemists encouraged not only to transmute base metals into gold but glass into gems?

Faith and ignorance can work wonders, and the very beautiful green glass bowl which can be seen in the Treasury of the Cathedral of San Lorenzo in Genoa (loot acquired at the sack of Caesarea in 1101 by a Genoese Crusader) was believed for centuries to be an emerald, variously described as the Holy Grail, a present from Solomon to the Queen of Sheba, or the dish which Salome presented to King Herod with the head of St John the Baptist upon it. Not all purchasers of imitation jewels in the past had accepted the situation without protest. When Salonina, wife of the Roman Emperor Gallienus (his eight years' reign lasted from AD 260 until 268) found that the jewels she had bought were made of glass, she demanded that the jeweller be thrown to the lions. The Emperor evidently considered her demand unreasonable for as the culprit stood in the arena waiting for death the cage was opened but, instead of a fierce lion, a loudly crowing cock strutted out.

In the distant past, colour was greatly admired, more so than during the seventeenth and eighteenth centuries

5 Drinking horn from Bingerbrück.
German, fifth century AD. British
Museum, London.

when the ideal seems to have been to purify the metal into a colourless brilliance. But that ambition arose late in the history of the craft and from the earliest times, by the addition of various oxides, much ingenuity has been spent in achieving a range of colours. With common bottle glass there was no problem—impurities in the silica tended to give it a greenish or brownish tone. For more sophisticated glass it was found that a turquoise-green and a turquoise-blue could be produced by the addition of copper. Iron stained green; cobalt blue; iron and antimony together, browns and yellows; manganese stained amethyst and purple.

A fine ruby-red was a later development thanks to the discovery in the late seventeenth century by Andreas Cassius that the addition of gold chloride had this result—one of the few European discoveries, incidentally, which was adopted by Chinese potters. Nineteenth-century developments were a black glass, derived from iron and manganese, and a greenish-yellow from uranium. Later still came yellow-browns thanks to titanium, red from selenium, purple and blue from nickel, yellowish-green from chromium. As for opaque white glass, usually known as milk- or milk-and-water glass, much in favour in the eighteenth century as a hopeful imitation of porcelain, that was produced by means of tin oxide, as

were the tin-enamelled wares of the potters which the Italians called maiolica, the French faience (from Faenza), the Dutch delft from the little city which was the centre of the industry, and ourselves English delftware. Another method is said to have been the addition of the ashes of calcined bones or of arsenic.

During the course of centuries there were, of course, triumphs and disasters, and for long periods it must have seemed as if the successes of the distant past—the technical successes—would never be repeated. Remember also that until the nineteenth century there was no such thing as scientific control; thermostats and similar neat devices were beyond imagination, progress was largely by guess and by God, and more hopeful experiments must have resulted in disaster than were ever brought to a successful conclusion. As the Roman Empire disintegrated, ancient skills deteriorated through lack of markets, for barbarian invaders were destructive and oafish and the sophisticated customers of the past were no longer there.

That is why, after nearly two thousand years, we still regard the Portland Vase not merely with admiration (for it is an astonishingly beautiful object) but with awe; the patience and sureness of touch of its unknown maker baffled everyone until in 1876 John Northwood at Stourbridge succeeded in making a satisfactory replica.

7

6 Small jug with the name of Tuthmosis III
on shoulder. Egyptian, *c.* 1504–1450 BC.
British Museum, London.

The technique is that of cutting through an opaque white outer casing, leaving the inner layer of dark glass (in this instance blue) to provide a contrasting background. This is cameo glass, which, in the glass centre of Stourbridge, was being taught in the local School of Design founded in 1852. The tradition was continued by John Northwood's son and nephews and was extended further by the Woodall brothers, George and Tom, with neat pretty-pretty designs in white against a pink or pink-brownish ground, by now expensive market darlings.

The best known of George Woodall's plates in cameo glass is the one which turned up in a sale at Sotheby's in 1926 when it made £140; it was next seen at auction in 1966 when the Corning Museum of Glass, New York, gave £7,600 for it. As to the Portland Vase itself, this was excavated in 1644 in a sarcophagus, probably that of the Emperor Severus, who was killed in AD 235. For many years it was one of the many treasures of the Barberini Palace in Rome and was, in the eighteenth century, bought for the Duchess of Portland. Her collection was sold in 1786 but the Duke purchased it at Christie's for 7,000 guineas, so it remained in the family. It was on loan to the British Museum when a lunatic smashed it in 1845; it was brilliantly repaired and finally became the property of the nation, just one hundred years later, for 30,000 guineas.

The newcomer to the study of glass, if he is to take an intelligent interest in subsequent developments, is recommended to look closely at this remarkable vessel and to use his imagination. Let him try to visualise the delicacy required from hand and eye to achieve it. First the vase itself – the blue glass – while still hot, would have been dipped into a crucible containing molten opaque white glass – in itself a tricky operation, for if the temperatures of two substances were too far apart the glass would crack and all would be ruined. If both inner vessel and its casing cooled satisfactorily, the carver had to cut away the outer layer of white opaque glass exactly as far as the inner layer, no more and no less, revealing part of the blue inner surface as required and also – and this would be the specially difficult portion of the operation – cutting at certain points in such a manner as to allow the underlying blue to show beneath the white and yet not be fully exposed so that the design would appear to have depths and shadows. The trouble is that when the technical difficulties were painstakingly – and expensively – mastered in the late nineteenth century, the best that could be devised in the way of design was so insipid and banal. Perhaps it should be noted here that Wedgwood made some famous replicas of the Portland Vase towards the close of the eighteenth century in his jasper ware – but that is, of course, an episode in the history of pottery, not of glass.

So much for the most surprising glass example from

8 Roman glass plaque moulded with a
design of Bacchanalian figures. Victoria
and Albert Museum, London.

9 Vase with collar of purple glass. Probably Syrian, third or fourth century AD. Victoria and Albert Museum, London.

10 Bowl of mosaic glass. Perhaps one of the much admired Murrhine bowls described by Pliny. Victoria and Albert Museum, London.

the ancient world; a few minor examples are known, but nothing of this quality. It is time to come down to earth and deal with more commonplace glass objects. Curious, by the way, that while Roman workpeople were capable of such outstanding and difficult operations, none of them until quite late (the fourth century AD) seems to have thought of using the far simpler method of engraving or cutting to enliven a plain glass surface, and then not often.

Considering its fragility and the violence of the centuries, it is surprising that so much has survived from Antiquity, for both Egyptian and Roman glass–that is, glass of the Roman world–turns up from time to time in the salerooms and some fine examples are scattered about in the museums and in a few private collections. On the whole, ancient Egyptian glass is a somewhat specialised taste–little vases and unguent bottles with simple decoration by means of threads of glass pressed into the body of the vessel before the finishing processes of grinding and polishing and coaxed into easy geometric patterns by means of a comb.

But the true glories of glass can scarcely be said to have begun until the technique of blown glass–and blown glass combined sometimes with moulding–was discovered at the beginning of the Christian era, for by this means a wonderful flexibility was possible and the viscous metal could be coaxed into many kinds of comely shapes. By chance it happened that this discovery was made when the known world was governed by a single central power, that of Rome, which enabled the skills

13

of the glass-workers of the Eastern Mediterranean to be transmitted easily enough to the borders of the Empire so that by the second century AD the reputation of the glassmen of Cologne and the Rhineland was no less than that of their tutors of Sidon and Alexandria.

The small bottles, flasks, vases and bowls, from whatever corner of the Roman world they have been found, and dating from the first four centuries of our era share, generally speaking, two things in common. They are nearly always comely objects, combining playfulness with feeling for form—a simple rather squat vase, for instance, decorated with a trailed blue network pattern or an amphora-shaped vessel, its two handles extending upwards in what can perhaps be described as a good-humoured wriggle. Shapes are nearly always elegant, as if their makers scarcely had to think about what they were doing but allowed their work to grow naturally.

The second point is haphazard; their visual appeal owes much to chance—to the chemical changes produced by many centuries of burial. The glass decays on the surface, light is broken up prismatically and the result is an attractive iridescence. If the vessel is immersed in water the iridescence vanishes, but it reappears as soon as the piece is dried. It is an agreeable phenomenon, not to be confused with the glass disease known in England as 'crizzling' which plagued late seventeenth-century glassmen.

As far as Western Europe is concerned, as the Roman Empire gradually succumbed to its own inefficiency and to attacks from beyond the Rhine and the Alps, the few glasses which have survived display an altogether rougher character. One can scarcely hope to own such a famous glass as the exquisite claw-beaker which was excavated in 1775 and the sole object buried with a skeleton at Castle Eden, Co. Durham—its colour green with blue trails at neck and base and on the upper row of claws. It can be dated to about AD 600 and was one of only nine glasses chosen to represent the Dark Ages (i.e. from about AD 450 to 900) in a notable exhibition in 1968 at the British Museum. It is sufficient to show that even in an age of confusion there were still craftsmen left who had ideas and could carry out quite a complicated design. All we know is that this beaker had been buried in the grave and so was clearly regarded as something very much out of the ordinary.

But the West had to wait several more centuries before glass-making could resume its ancient prosperity. Only the Eastern Empire, with its capital at Constantinople, could provide the necessary stability for a flourishing market and patronise the highly skilled glassmen of the Eastern Mediterranean. But even that marvellous, if narrow, civilisation was destined to become more and more harassed by its enemies from both North and East, until finally subjugated by a fiercely vigorous conqueror. Europe had to restart from scratch.

12 Roman hexagonal bluish-green jar
found in Cologne. Roman, first or second
century BC. Victoria and Albert Museum,
London.

A Gleam of Light

The rebirth of the European glass industry seems to have occurred in the most unlikely of places—the group of islands which became known as Venice and which developed from the rude huts of a few refugees from barbarian incursions from the North to the extraordinary city as we know it today and which, though its glory and independence have long departed, can still stir the imagination and even, in spite of its record of hard-headed and hard-hearted commercialism, can occasionally touch the heart.

There were glass furnaces in the city by the eleventh century until, owing to the danger from fires, the Council of Ten banished the glassmen to the island of Murano two hundred years later (1291). There they have remained ever since, still a great tourist attraction and producing some admirable modern work, though no longer dominating the glass trade. Originally their skill must have owed a great deal to refugees from the near East, and the outrageous Crusader plus Venetian Sack of Constantinople in 1204 no doubt brought many others with a further influx when the Turks overwhelmed the city in 1453.

Whatever the exact circumstances, the industry flourished and for many years enjoyed a near monopoly of the European market. The Most Serene Republic provided security in troubled times, but was in no way benevolent. It imposed heavy penalties upon runaway workmen and did all it could to discourage the dissemination of knowledge which might in any way harm its exceedingly profitable trade. None the less, many highly skilled men, whether discontented or merely adventurous, did escape from time to time, most of them to the Netherlands.

England has to thank one of these exiles, who came over to London from Antwerp in the reign of Elizabeth I, for the foundation of a viable glass industry. An enterprising Lorrainer, Jean Carré—a businessman, not a technician—obtained a licence to manufacture glass in 1567 *à la façon de Venise*; Jacopo Verzelini arrived in 1571 to manage Carré's glass-house in Crutched Friars, made a considerable fortune, retired in 1592 and lived until 1606. We are in debt to Carré, who died in about 1572, both for Verzelini and for his previous encouragement of several families of his fellow Lorrainers who also settled in England and, after working first in the well-wooded Weald of Surrey and Kent eventually moved north to Stourbridge. Their names deserve to be remembered. Du Thisac was anglicised as Tyzack, de Hennezel as Henzey, De Thiétry as Tittery, De Houx as Hoe. But the Weald men worked in the old tradition of forest glass *(Waldglas)*; the Italians were more sophisticated.

The main flood of Venetian escapees seems to have been directed to the Spanish Netherlands, but there was another centre of glass expertise in Italy, by this time almost forgotten, but which, in its day, must have had a very great influence in spreading knowledge of the craft far and wide. This was Altare, a quiet little place just off the road from Genoa to Turin, which still contains one glass-house making ordinary commercial products from fish bowls to drinking glasses. The extraordinary thing about the village is the strength of its traditions, for men are working there today whose ancestors came to Altare about the year 1000 from Flanders—members of seven families whose Italian names reveal their origin; thus Bourdon became Bordoni, Saroud Saroldi and so on.

Later, members of eight Venetian families joined the group, later still two others, and all combined together to form *L'Università dell'Arte Vitrea* (The Society of Glass-making). Documents in the library at Savona give a slightly different account saying that the Altarists came originally from Normandy and Brittany even earlier, but the present glassmen in Altare say that this is not the case. Whatever is the truth of the matter, it is certain that they were given titles of nobility on several occasions by the Marchese di Monferrato, in whose territory Altare is situated, and that they obtained the necessary potash from the forest surrounding them.

The remarkable thing about them is that, unlike the Venetians, they were not harassed by narrow government or guild restrictions; indeed, their organisation seems to have been exceptionally enlightened and made no objection to its workpeople travelling far afield; a statute of 1495 actually encourages emigration. The country which profited chiefly from this was France, but they were to be found elsewhere also, and it is of interest to note that, in addition to the customary phrase '*à la façon de Venise*' the words '*à la façon des Sieurs Altaristes*' also occurs in sixteenth-century documents.

It will be clear from all this that the rest of Europe owes much of its glass know-how to Italians, whether runaway Venetians or outward-looking Altarists. It follows also that whether a man was working in Spain, for instance, or in the Netherlands, he could scarcely be expected to produce glasses in anything but his usual style, and consequently that today's collectors must be satisfied, more often than not, to have their possessions catalogued vaguely as *façon de Venise*. Craftsmen from Murano were working at Antwerp by 1541; volunteers from Altare were staffing a glass-house at Liège in 1569.

One may sum up by asserting that during the thousand years since the collapse of the Roman Empire, Europe made do with what was remembered of the age-old techniques of the distant past. By the sixteenth century far more sophisticated methods had been devised, among them a means of purifying the metal and of manipulating it with greater flexibility. The credit for this must be given to Italians irrespective of their place of origin; it was they who laid the foundations, it was they who taught others their skills.

16

13, 64

14 Emerald green marriage goblet.
Venetian, second half of the fifteenth
century. British Museum, London.

15 Sapphire blue standing cup painted
with Venus procession. Venetian, mid
fifteenth century. British Museum,
London.

16 English diamond-engraved goblet by
Verzelini, 1581. Victoria and Albert
Museum, London.

17 Colourless glass boat or 'nef' ewer,
attributed to Ermonia Vivarini. Venetian,
sixteenth century. British Museum,
London.

The earliest glass which can be ascribed to Verzelini
16 is dated 1577 and belongs to the Corning Museum of
Glass, New York; altogether about nine glasses have
survived, incorporating the characteristic hollow knop
in the stem. The metal is, of course, soda metal, faintly
greenish, and is decorated with diamond-point engraving, attributed to a Frenchman, Anthony de Lisle,
who applied for naturalisation in 1597. Verzelini also
became naturalised as soon as he was able to secure a
twenty-one year monopoly from Elizabeth I of the right to
manufacture glass *à la façon de Venise*. This he did despite 13, 64
the intrigues of jealous importers and manufacturing
rivals.

In England, as elsewhere, the monopoly system was a
blessing to an industry struggling to make itself efficient
and a curse later on, for it stifled competition. The
monarchy, always short of cash, not unnaturally
approved of it as a means of raising the wind, and glass

manufacture suffered from it for a further century or so.

Verzelini and his successors evidently enjoyed a fashionable demand, for the best people, a little bored by silver, became anxious to patronise the glassmen (whether they worked in Venice or England), the well-off who were socially beneath them followed suit in the hope of keeping up with the Joneses, while those at the bottom of the social pyramid, who could not afford glasses 13,64 *à la façon de Venise*, made do with ordinary forest glass instead of rough pottery beakers or leather bottles.

The evidence is provided by the observant Harrison in his *Description of England 1586*: 'It is a world to see in these our daies, wherein gold and silver most aboundeth, how that our gentilitie as lothing those metals (because of the plentie) do now choose rather the Venice glasses, both for our wine and beere . . . such is the nature of man generallie, that it most coveteth things difficult to be atteined . . . And as this is seen in the gentilitie, so in the wealthy communaltie the like desire for glass is not neglected . . . The poorest also will have glasse if they may; but sith the Venetian is somewhat too deere for them, they content themselves with such as are made at home of ferne and burned stone.' As a side-light upon late sixteenth-century standards of living this is exceptionally illuminating.

After the retirement of Verzelini, the records of glass manufacture in England remain decidedly obscure for nearly a century. We know broad outlines but very few details; we know the names of the holders of various licences, but next to nothing as to the glass they made. Nor were these men interested in glass; they were in the business for what they could make of it, financiers rather than manufacturers, and, taking a judicious view of the historical background, he will be an unduly prejudiced critic who would venture to assert that they were a disaster.

One of them particularly, Sir Robert Mansell, a retired admiral, efficient and ruthless—a typical organisation man—can be regarded as very nearly a blessing, just the type necessary for difficult times. That they *were* difficult is scarcely open to question, for the Government had long been alarmed by the steady depletion of the forests in Surrey, Sussex and Kent, thanks to the demands of iron-masters and glassmen, and at length, in 1615, the use of wood fuel was forbidden by royal proclamation, presenting the trade with a crisis.

It would, no doubt, have been solved in any case but the chief architect of new methods—that is the use of coal from Tyneside and Scotland and the Forest of Dean—was Mansell who, by 1618, had bought out his partners and remained monopolist *par excellence* until his death in 1656. He must have been a formidable personage; at first he brought coal down from the mines in the Kingdom of Fife, and then, when Scottish shipmasters raised their charges to what he considered impossible heights, he transferred his affections to Tyneside. By 1620 he was in control of practically every worthwhile glass-house in the country, assisted by the no less formidable and competent Lady Mansell who was left in sole charge while the admiral, recalled to the Service, took time off to command an expedition to curb the ambitions of the Barbary pirates in the Mediterranean. He was the unquestionable master of the trade until the Civil War, which put an end to the monopoly system and also to the life of Charles I who, sinking further and further into debt, relied upon it throughout his reign to provide him with funds, which an obstinate Parliament so frequently refused.

It is fair to guess that, by about 1650, the year after the King's execution, the glass-makers scattered around the country were able to work more or less as they wished, though for an impoverished market, without the risks of legal penalties. The system of licences returned with the Restoration in 1660, but with less rigidity. For a few brief years George Villiers, 2nd Duke of Buckingham, obtained a licence to manufacture mirrors at Vauxhall and table glass at Greenwich. Again he was no glassman, but a financier, and not without a kind of easy-going guile, for when professional glass technicians attempted to obtain, or succeeded in obtaining, a licence, he seems to have bought them up and employed them instead of browbeating them. To what extent his excursion into the glass world was profitable is not known, nor is it possible *with absolute* certainty to attribute any glasses to his men.

But times were changing and the English trade was soon to escape from its dependence upon Venetian fashions and Venetian know-how. At about the same time German and Bohemian glass-makers, by a different route, reached a similar independence. Both in metal content and in form the two sections of the glass industry differed considerably, neither taking much notice of the other, but each made its own contribution to the decline of Venice. This must be discussed later.

Meanwhile, as proof of the ascendency of Venice, up till nearly the end of the seventeenth century, we have preserved in the British Museum the records of a firm of glass-sellers, John Greene and Michael Measey. They imported from Allesio Morelli of Murano between 1667 and 1672 over one thousand looking-glass plates and two thousand dozen glasses. There is a continuous series of complaints about quality and breakages, until in 1671 there is a warning that if things went on like this they might have to look round for supplies at home. By this time the firm, prominent in the Glass Sellers Company, was no doubt aware of future plans. Two years later, with the backing of the Company, George Ravenscroft 22, 29 set up his experimental glass-house at Henley (employing Italian craftsmen as his assistants), and, as far as England was concerned, the New Age had begun.

18 This miniature from a Czech
manuscript of The Travels of Sir John
Mandeville shows the primitive equipment
used in a glass-works until the seventeenth
century. British Museum, London.

The New Age

England and the German-speaking Lands

19 Glass and cover, painted with a Spanish equestrian figure. Perhaps enamelled in Nuremberg. German, second half of the seventeenth century. Victoria and Albert Museum, London.

20 English covered goblet. Late seventeenth century. Victoria and Albert Museum, London.

The breakthrough to a new type of glass in England is reasonably well documented and, by surviving examples, it is possible to trace the steps by which it was developed. The Glass Sellers Company provided the financial backing, George Ravenscroft (1618-81) the technical brains and the determination necessary to bring his experiments to success. He set up his experimental glass-house in the Savoy in 1673, employing Italians to assist him. The progress made must have seemed satisfactory to his hard-headed business associates, for they decided to invest further, financing a new series of experiments at a new glass-house at Henley-on-Thames. The first results were an imperfect glass-of-lead, that is a glass containing lead oxide. This was found liable to 'crizzle' (to become obscured by a multitude of fine interior cracks) thanks probably to the use of overmuch alkali. This defect he overcame by the addition of yet more lead, and, having got his ingredients right, the way was clear.

At this point it is necessary to clear up a confusing use of words. Oxide of lead had been used in early times, especially in coloured imitation gems, whose brilliance it enhanced, but never in vessels for the table. In any case, its use in the distant past demanded only about one per cent, whereas in English glass of the closing years of the seventeenth century it could be as much as a quarter of the whole weight. The term 'lead glass' or 'glass-of-lead' was now firmly established. Unfortunately the words 'flint glass' were also introduced, probably because powdered English flints began to be used as substitutes for imported Venetian pebbles, while potash was the alkali. Very soon ordinary sand replaced flint in English practice, but the two terms were used indiscriminately to the confusion of beginners. They describe exactly the same product.

It is presumed that Ravenscroft and his backers were at first merely anxious to find a formula which would enable them to make a glass equal to the Venetian, so that they would no longer be dependent upon imports. In the end they produced not just a substitute, but glass of a wholly different nature. Venetian glass was rather horny and could be blown out very thin. English lead glass was very much heavier, with an oily brilliance and a remarkable capacity to disperse light, far more than the natural rock-crystal upon which every glass-maker had set his eyes for centuries as the ideal pattern to follow.

Ravenscroft in 1673 was granted a patent for seven years for the manufacture of 'a new sort of crystalline glass resembling rock crystal'. By 1676 it was reported to the Company that 'the defect of the flint glasses (which were formerly observed to crissel and decay)' had been remedied. In the same year it was agreed that the new glasses should bear a seal which, at this stage, was Ravenscroft's own device of a raven's head. A certain Hawley Bishop carried on at Henley and it was he who

took over the Savoy house after Ravenscroft's death in 1681. The new glass had arrived and by the close of the century was fully in command of the market, for nearly a hundred glass-houses were making it. It was a technical revolution which ensured the prosperity of the industry for a century. For the first time English glasses were made of a characteristic metal owing nothing to outside influences and they also acquired a style of their own which makes them unmistakable.

Just as Italian experience, whether from Venice or Altare, was essential for the foundation of the English glass industry, other countries—Spain, France and the German-speaking lands North of the Alps—were no less indebted to it. Spain and France, though generally imposing their own forms, did not, on the whole, vary much from Italian practice; much of their output during many years could be classified as a kind of international 13, 64 *façon de Venise*, as was so much of that produced by the glass-houses of Antwerp.

26

Silesia and Bohemia, however, were more enterprising 24, 25 and though they had at first to rely upon southern craftsmen, they began to evolve a definitely national glass body at about the same time as Ravenscroft succeeded in perfecting his lead glass. This became known as Bohemian crystal. It is likely that the first experiments, as in England, were directed towards a mere imitation of current Venetian imports so as to become independent. But, as in England, the result was a new type, achieved not by the addition of lead, but of chalk and by the use of potash instead of soda. The new glass was brilliant and well suited to engraving; once the formula was established it became widely known and was soon in use all over Germany. What is more, it held its own easily enough against quite formidable competition.

Venetian glass, though called *cristallo* in emulation of the greatly admired rock-crystal, still remained slightly smoky or pale yellow and, by about the year 1700, could not be said to be the equal of either the English or

German variety. Its appeal from now on, and for many years, lay more in the fantasy of its forms and in the manual dexterity of its workpeople than in the quality of the glass itself.

The glass produced by this new formula throughout Bohemia, Silesia and in the various eighteenth-century German states, was looked upon as having been a divine gift to the lapidary. By 1680 there was already an established tradition of engraving on glass, its earliest and most famous practitioner, Kaspar Lehman, a notable jewel-cutter who had been summoned to Prague in the early years of the seventeenth century by that great Habsburg patron of the arts, the Emperor Rudolf II, and was there encouraged to use his skill upon glass; a grateful monarch bestowed upon him a title of nobility in 1609.

A distinctive Bohemian style is recognisable from about 1680 onwards, mostly dignified thick-walled goblets and covers, often fluted and decorated with engravings. These were of several sorts – views of towns, allegories of Peace and War, engravings of ships or of traders' wagons or, rarely, an occasional historical souvenir such as a goblet with an equestrian portrait of the Emperor Leopold I and the Sultan Mustapha II, to commemorate a peace treaty with Turkey. Another event which rankled for years was the seizure of Silesia by the enterprising, unlovable pirate, Frederick the Great, in 1742; some unknown glassman engraved a goblet with the imperial two-headed eagle and allegorical figures of Bohemia and Silesia.

Certain types of vessel and certain techniques are peculiar to these wide regions. Occasionally work from particular localities can be identified, such as the noble goblet carved in rock-crystal style (the German term is *Hochschnitt*) in the form of a cornucopia. This can be dated about 1700 and was seen at Sotheby's some years ago in the Beck Collection – a magnificent, exuberant example; it is from the glass-works owned by the Counts

24 Beaker with hunting scene. The names of the Silesian nobles are engraved with diamond-point. Bohemian or Silesian, c. 1600. Museum für Kunst und Gewerbe, Hamburg.

25 Clear glass tumbler with engraving cut through ruby flash. Bohemian, c. 1840. Victoria and Albert Museum, London.

26 (Left) Glass tankard. German, 1679, and (Right) Milchglas cup painted with figures in a landscape by Johann Schaper, c. 1670. Victoria and Albert Museum, London.

24

25

26

27

28 Amethyst coloured jug. Probably Bristol, *c.* 1790. Collection: L. M. Bickerton, Esq.

29 English jug, boldly ribbed with rope-like handle, by George Ravenscroft, 1675–80. Victoria and Albert Museum, London.

30 Bakers' and Ropemakers' beaker of Gottfried Berger and Caspar Hein. Probably Central German, 1697. Museum für Kunst und Gewerbe, Hamburg.

28

29

30

Schaffgotsch in the valley of the Riesengebirge in Silesia. Needless to add that not all glasses of this period are quite up to this standard.

Another method of glass decoration seems to have come into fashion about halfway through the seventeenth century–*Schwarzlot*, enamel painting mainly in black, first devised, it seems, by Johann Schaper (1621–70), a free-lance painter on both glass and pottery, a combination of roles which was by no means uncommon. A third method, difficult, highly decorative and inevitably expensive, is *Zwischengoldglas*, which is engraved gold-leaf between two layers of glass. The goblets and beakers made in this technique, and which have survived the years, are among the most engaging things which have come down to us, at once good-humoured and dignified. Apart from goblets and beakers, popular shapes were the *Humpen*, a large size beaker, and *Stangenglas* (pole glass), a tall cylindrical beaker with spreading foot. When this vessel was encircled by a spiral thread dividing it in roughly equal parts, it was known as a *Passglas*; a guest would be required to drink down to one of these lines before passing it on. This was, of course, a beer-drinking country which evolved the types of glass most suited to the enjoyment of the 'wine of the country'.

26

27

31 Three dark brown sealed wine bottles;
seventeenth and eighteenth centuries.
Worthing Museum, Sussex.

But coming down from these rather expensive heights to day-by-day life on earth, one is bound to catch up with the humble, but useful and by no means inelegant *Roemer,* seen in dozens of homely Dutch seventeenth-century still lifes – a nice, comforting shape, its origin going way back at least to medieval times, and almost invariably carried out in greenish forest glass – its modern variants as popular as ever in the Rhine Valley and the Netherlands. The normal type is that with a fairly wide bowl, curving inwards slightly at the rim, and a hollow stem decorated with applied 'prunts' for greater safety in holding it.

The area from the North Sea to Bohemia is, of course, immense, and it is usually impossible to identify the productions of any particular region with any degree of exactitude. As elsewhere, glassmen were inclined to be rovers not altogether because of a basically restless temperament, but because they were continuously short of wood fuel for their furnaces; this in itself would make accurate identification difficult. Given that and the ambitions of the best technicians, it is not surprising that differences in quality and in colour have been noticed in the output of a single glass-house during a single decade. It is only later, in the eighteenth century,

that one can hope to identify glasses from a few of the multitude of glass-houses which were operating over this vast expanse of country. The forests of Hesse, east of the Rhine, were lively centres; yet more important were the wooded mountains and valleys of the borders of Silesia and Bohemia (for instance the Riesengebirge), the Bavarian Böhmer Wald and several districts in Saxony and Thuringia.

International highway robbery of the past two centuries and more, beginning with the rape of Silesia in 1742, has bedevilled the history of the European glass industry to such a degree, that it is difficult to steer a straight course amid national rivalries. Both the modern Czechoslovakia and Austria have suffered grievously in our own day and many fine things have been attributed to Bohemian glass-houses when they were, in fact, directed from Austria in the days of the Austrian Empire. As far as possible I have tried to ignore these unhappy events; this is not political history, but the story of how glass manufacture began and survived in spite of interference.

The Netherlands

32 Stippled wineglass with faceted stem,
engraved in the manner of David Wolff.
Netherlands, seventeenth century.
Christie Manson and Woods Limited,
London.

33 Goblet with purple bowl and foot, and
stem colourless with twisted opaque white,
blue and red threads. Netherlands, early
seventeenth century. British Museum,
London.

34 A Netherlands armorial goblet with
round-funnel bowl solid at the base and
containing air beads. Sold at auction in
1971 at Sotheby and Company, London,
for £80 ($196).

For most of us, the idea of the kind of glasses which were in ordinary use on and around the Lower Rhine is derived from Dutch and Flemish pictures, whose painters took great pleasure in depicting tables heaped with good food, and who were fascinated by the manner in which windows and objects in other parts of the room were reflected on the curved surfaces of the wine glasses. One is tempted to jump to the conclusion that such glasses were made in the land to which the paintings belong, but this would be too large an assumption, for the *Roemer* was the common wine glass over a vast area, and there were plenty of glass-houses over the border in Germany, who produced it. We are on no less unsure ground in the case of the numerous slender Italianate glasses, which are seen in the paintings as often as are the *Roemers*. One wonders whether they were imports from Venice, or made by Italian workmen in Antwerp, or Amsterdam, or Liège, or Italian-instructed workmen there, or in a dozen other centres in the neighbourhood.

There were workmen at Antwerp by 1541 who had escaped from Murano, and by the end of the sixteenth century, the craft had spread to Liège, Amsterdam and many other places. One can say, that throughout the seventeenth and eighteenth centuries there was nothing to distinguish the glass of the Netherlands from that of their neighbours, apart from its decoration. This is partly because it was taken up by amateurs as well as by professionals, and whether it was wheel-engraved or decorated in diamond-point, it reached a remarkably high standard.

We cannot account for this amateur interest—it is a phenomenon which does not appear elsewhere—but there were at least three Dutch women, who achieved a modicum of fame through this unusual sparetime occupation. They were Anna Roemers Visscher, who died aged 64 in 1651, and her sister, Maria, who died in 1649—the daughters of an Amsterdam merchant—and a younger contemporary, Anna Maria van Schurman, who died in 1692. All three used diamond-point. So did Willem van Heemskerk of Leyden (1603–92) who engraved many pieces between 1648 and 1690, one of them an elegant bottle, signed and dated 1674, in a beautiful flowing calligraphy and bearing a couplet in praise of wine. Another master of the diamond-point was Willem Mooleyser—several glasses by him, dated between 1685 and 1697, have survived and there is one in the Victoria and Albert Museum decorated with the arms of the United Netherlands, and of William III as King of Great Britain and Ireland, dated April 19th 1689 (that is, only eight days after the joint coronation of William and Mary).

The eighteenth century saw the introduction into the Netherlands of wheel-engraving, a much coarser method, and it is thought mostly the work of German craftsmen. The glasses used were frequently English, because the English glass-of-lead was so lustrous and displayed engraving to such effect. Popular subjects were shipping—a launch, for instance, would be recorded with a suitable inscription—weddings, or betrothals. But the diamond-point was not forgotten entirely, and some of the most delightful of Dutch engraved glasses—and some of the rarest—are decorated in stipple—a very slow but rewarding method (practised today by Laurence Whistler) in which the picture is built up by the diamond-point being set in a handle which is struck by a hammer; the result, a series of dots, and graphically described by W. B. Honey as if 'the engraving was resting like a scarcely perceptible film breathed upon the glass'. Yet another amateur is credited with the introduction of this stipple engraving on glass, Frans Greenwood (1680–1761), who was employed by the Municipality of Dordrecht. It was a fashion which lasted well into the middle of the nineteenth century. Its best-known exponent during the last half of the eighteenth century was a certain David Wolff (1732–98).

Italy

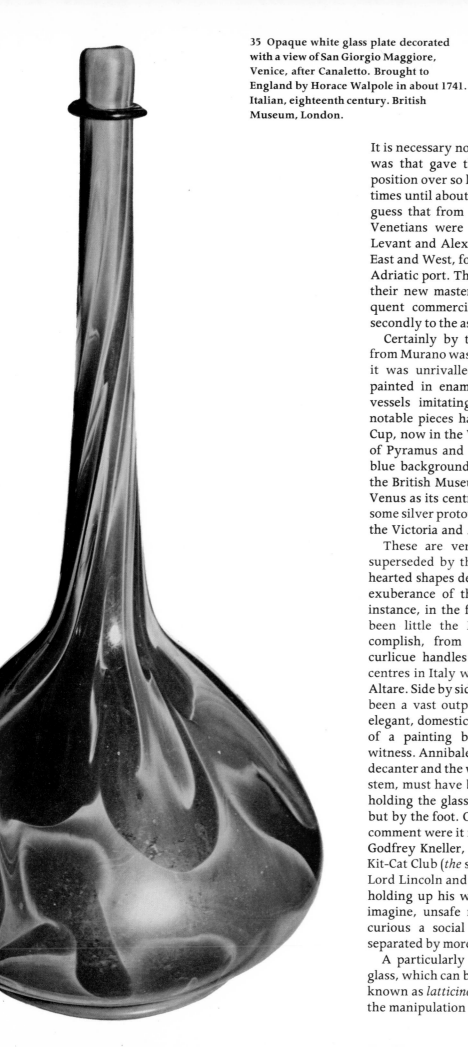

35 Opaque white glass plate decorated with a view of San Giorgio Maggiore, Venice, after Canaletto. Brought to England by Horace Walpole in about 1741. Italian, eighteenth century. British Museum, London.

36 Long-necked bottle imitating chalcedony. Italian, *c.* 1600. Victoria and Albert Museum, London.

It is necessary now to go back a little and see just what it was that gave the Italian glassmen their pre-eminent position over so lengthy a period—that is, from medieval times until about the year 1700. It is not unreasonable to guess that from the time of the Crusades onwards the Venetians were in contact with the glassmen of the Levant and Alexandria and that many, caught between East and West, found it expedient to migrate to the great Adriatic port. They possessed the knowledge and found their new masters appreciated their skill; their subsequent commercial success was due to this first and secondly to the astute business sense of the Republic.

Certainly by the end of the fifteenth century glass from Murano was admired far and wide; by the sixteenth it was unrivalled. Colour was used frequently, both painted in enamels on clear or coloured glass, or in vessels imitating precious stones like agate. A few notable pieces have survived, among them the Fairfax 40 Cup, now in the Victoria and Albert Museum—the story of Pyramus and Thisbe in enamels against a turquoise blue background—and an enchanting nuptial goblet in the British Museum, depicting a jovial procession, with Venus as its central figure. There are others based upon some silver prototype, like a splendid goblet and cover in the Victoria and Albert Museum.

These are very decidedly of their day and were superseded by the seventeenth-century fanciful, light-hearted shapes depending less upon form than upon the exuberance of their makers—stems of wine cups, for instance, in the form of serpents. There seems to have been little the Murano glass-blowers could not accomplish, from glass ships to fantastic knops and curlicue handles; nor have we any proof that other centres in Italy were not equally accomplished, notably Altare. Side by side with so much fantasy there must have been a vast output of down to earth, yet wonderfully elegant, domestic wares, to which the colour illustration of a painting by Annibale Carracci bears eloquent 42 witness. Annibale died in 1609, so this admirably shaped decanter and the wine glass, with its wide bowl and short stem, must have been made before that date. The boy is holding the glass in a very odd way—not by the stem, but by the foot. One could easily pass that over without comment were it not for the fact that in a painting by Sir Godfrey Kneller, of about 1710, of two members of the Kit-Cat Club (*the* snob club of the reign of Queen Anne)—Lord Lincoln and the Duke of Newcastle—one of them is holding up his wine glass in the same, and one would imagine, unsafe manner. How can we account for so curious a social habit in two such different circles separated by more than a century?

A particularly attractive method of decorating clear glass, which can be definitely credited to Murano, is that known as *latticino*, a convenient single word to describe 38 the manipulation of straight or spirally arranged threads

39 Painted armorial dish. Venetian,
c. 1600. Victoria and Albert Museum.
London.

40 The Fairfax Cup. A semi-opaque turquoise glass beaker painted in enamel colours and gilt. It is one of three glasses with enamel decoration on turquoise and is the only one with figures in which different episodes of a single classical legend are unfolded in sequence round the bowl. It tells the story of Pyramus and Thisbe from Ovid, Metamorphoses, Book IV (better known perhaps to English readers from A Midsummer Night's Dream) in three scenes. The one shown on this side is of Pyramus, followed by Thisbe, setting out for their trysting-place by the well—shown as a Renaissance fountain. The beaker belonged to the Fairfax family from before 1643. Venetian, late fifteenth century. Victoria and Albert Museum, London.

of opaque glass embedded in the clear glass. The technique depended entirely upon the skill of the glass-blower and was capable of nearly infinite variety – the more intricate geometrical patterns produced by this means were known as lace glass (*vetro de trina*). The fashion had a long life, more than two hundred years, for it was in favour, as far as can be discovered, in the middle of the sixteenth century, and was still much admired towards the end of the eighteenth. A certain Giuseppe Briati, who died in 1772, specialised in it. Examples are seen in the auction rooms from time to time but, as with so many other delectable glasses from the past, one is hard put to it to decide whether they are the work of Murano craftsmen in Venice, the work of expatriate Italians elsewhere, or from a dozen glass-houses up and down Europe manned by workpeople who had learnt their skill from Italian emigrants. Cataloguers, in default of the clearest evidence, are commendably cautious, classifying such glasses as often as not as '*Façon de Venise,* perhaps Netherlandish'.

As tourists – at first rather grand persons, or at least young sprigs of the nobility bear-led by the family tutor – began to haunt Venice, the city, always with an eye to business, was not slow in fostering a trade in souvenirs, not only views by painters of the calibre of Canaletto and his followers, but more humble anonymous craftsmen working in glass. The best known of these souvenirs must be the plate which Horace Walpole brought back with him from Venice in 1741, now in the British Museum. It is a view of S. Giorgio Maggiore after a 35 painting by Canaletto – red monochrome against a background of white opaque glass. As elsewhere, white opaque glass, commonly known as milk-glass, became popular during the eighteenth century, thanks to the flood of porcelain of all kinds. At a distance milk-glass, painted in enamels, is no bad substitute, though 37, 38 considerably lighter, and was made as enthusiastically in Venice, Bristol and Stourbridge as it was in China. The myriad tourist souvenirs of the nineteenth and twentieth centuries can claim a not undistinguished ancestry.

North America

There seem to be only the vaguest references to, and no convincing glasses from the few struggling glass-houses of the seventeenth and early eighteenth centuries in the vast area destined to become the United States. The earliest concern of which we have definite knowledge is that of Wistar's, which made window glass and bottles at Wistarburg near Salem in New Jersey and which functioned with modest success from about 1739 to 1775. Similar commercial products were produced by the Glass House Company of New York (*c.* 1752–67) and by the Germanstown Works near Boston (1753–68). So far records exist of only two pre-Revolution firms which attempted to make table glass–H. W. Stiegel's second glass-house at Manheim, Penn. and the Philadelphia Glass Works at Kensington, but inevitably both also produced run-of-the-mill bottle and window glass as a necessary insurance against financial disaster. Between 1772 and 1777 tableware had become important at Kensington and between 1769 and 1774 at Manheim, and each place claimed to be the first to have manufactured clear lead (or flint) glass. In 1771 the American Philosophical Society reported that the Stiegel pieces inspected by them were 'equal in beauty and quality to the generality of Flint Glass imported from England'.

After the Revolution, during the years from 1783 to 1824, about twenty-four furnaces were built, the most important that of the Pittsburgh Glass Works (1824), the first in America to burn coal, and that was the year in which Congress imposed a tariff which was increased in 1828 and 1832. The earliest of the post-Revolution houses was that of J. F. Amelung and Co. near Frederick, Maryland, which lasted from 1785 to 1795 and produced a certain amount of non-lead domestic glass following European fashions, of which a few pieces have been identified–or attributed–together with certain engraved presentation pieces.

A very great commercial, though not an aesthetic advance, was due to the invention by 1829 of the technique of pressed glass–that is, a method by which molten metal is dropped into a mould and a plunger is rammed in, forcing the glass to all parts of the mould. Glasses made by this means were first produced commercially at Sandwich, Massachusetts and the method, which cut costs to a remarkable extent, was soon in operation generally, reaching England in 1833. According to Deming Jarves, founder of the Boston and Sandwich Glass Works, by 1852 this American invention had so reduced production costs that consumption had increased tenfold during those thirty years.

The ancient craft was becoming mechanised, but the enormous size of the country, its expansion westwards, its poor communications at this period, favoured a certain local individuality, so that in Middle Western areas it is possible to detect, amid the ordinary output of bottle and window glass, the continued survival of

45

48

47 A pair of unusual American vases with red, white and blue stripes applied in the Venetian manner. The globular covers are known as 'witch balls'. Characteristic of some of the best work by the New England Glass Company, about 1840. The Metropolitan Museum of Art, New York. Edgar J. Kaufmann Charitable Foundation Fund.

48 American blown pattern-moulded flasks made in the Midwest, *c.* 1820–40. Yale University Art Gallery, the Mabel Brady Garvan Collection, New Haven, Connecticut.

blown-glass vessels—jugs and so forth—blown by the age-old process for regional use. The Eastern glass-houses were inevitably anchored more firmly to European traditions, though it is doubtful whether their makers were fully conscious of their debt; what is certain is that, on the whole, they followed at several removes the stylistic mannerisms of European glass (mostly Bohemian and German) and, within this tradition, evolved what American collectors today call a distinctive folk style.

While it is correct that no glass has survived which is definitely of the seventeenth century, there are references to certain pioneer attempts, the earliest of them at Jamestown, Virginia, where Captain John Smith and his little band of optimistic settlers, observing the abundance of both sand and forest, built a glass-house with the aid of eight Dutch and Polish glass-workers in 1608, but this venture seems to have failed quite soon, for when Captain Argall arrived in 1617 as Governor, the buildings had fallen into decay. A second attempt was made in 1621, with six Italians controlled by a Captain William Norton. They were provided with shelter while the looked around for a site which would be safe from a surprise attack; they seem to have been successful, for the Italians survived the Jamestown massacre of 1622 and the site of their glass-house has been discovered about three-quarters of a mile from the original settlement. The Dutch established a glass-house in New York during the seventeenth century, that is, before 1664, while they were in control of the settlement and, in a letter of 1683, William Penn mentions a Pennsylvanian glass-house.

In none of these meagre records is there any indication of the kind of glass manufactured. In the conditions of that day it is most unlikely anything was attempted beyond ordinary bottle and window glass. That the latter was made at Philadelphia is indicated by a brief record of the employment of 'a broad glass man' (broad glass = window glass) and Joshua Tittery, from New-castle-on-Tyne, evidently a member of the family of De Thiétry (anglicised into Tittery) which, with many other glassmen from Lorraine, came to England in 1567, introduced by Jean Carré of Arras under privilege from Queen Elizabeth I. Two glass-houses are recorded in New York in 1732. One of them was known as the 'Glass House Farm'; it appears on De Witt's *Farm Map of New York* facing the Hudson, near what is now 35th Street. The other was an enterprise with four partners who made an agreement with J. M. Greiner of Saxe-Weimar, Germany, to come over, remain twenty years and teach them the 'Art and Mystery of Erecting and Building a Glass House and allso in Blowing and Making of Glass'. The company remained in operation until 1767, but here again its products have not been identified—which brings us again to the foundation of the Wistar concern, the first of the known glass-houses which had any substantial success.

Wistar had crossed the Atlantic in 1717 at the age of twenty-one; he was German, and he was followed by hundreds of his fellow countrymen. Inevitably styles were those in fashion in eighteenth-century Germany. He was an entrepreneur, not a glassman, and he began operations by hiring four experts (all with German names) and paid their passage money from Rotterdam. His agreement with them was that they were to teach him and his son their skills while he provided their keep, the furnace, etc., and one third of the profits. The site of his works has been excavated, but only the coarsest kind of glass fragments found. However, he advertised such things as spirit bottles and snuff bottles—both would have been of square section—so it has been suggested that such things might have been made, not as part of his ordinary commercial productions, but were vessels made by his men for their own use or for presents—things outside the normal boring run of the place, done partly for their amusement and to keep their hand in. There was another glass-house at Germanstown, Mass., also manned by Germans, a concern which, in spite of a disastrous fire in 1755, was still in operation five years later.

But all these were very small beginnings designed primarily to provide the Colonies with basic glass necessities—bottles and windows. The first serious attempt to emulate the fine, clear table glass imported from England (lead glass, flint glass) or from the European Continent (soda-lime glass) was made during the 1760s by Henry William Stiegel, a native of Cologne, who landed in Philadelphia in 1750, aged twenty-one, took a job with Jacob Huber, the owner of an ironworks, and married his master's daughter. Within six years both father and daughter had died and Stiegel found himself in control.

American expert opinion is extremely cautious in attributing any known vessel to the Stiegel glass-house, and prefers to speak only of 'Stiegel type' glass. With this warning in our ears it is possible, none the less, to be reasonably certain as to the range of his table glass—from a smooth, clear, English-type flint glass of good quality (witness the opinion of the members of the American Philosophical Society already quoted) through various engraved, coloured and enamelled pieces, the decoration largely German and not at all sophisticated. Decidedly American, and not made in Europe, are small rounded pocket flasks which can well be attributed to his men (at one time he employed one hundred and thirty) and he also made bowls, cream jugs, etc., in blue, purple, amethyst and emerald green, blown-moulded, as were inexpensive vessels of the sort in England—and very attractive they can be with their twisted ribbing, wherever made.

Stiegel, besides being adventurous, was clearly a character quite out of the ordinary, as colourful as his glass. His enterprise at Manheim, paid for partly by the

49 American pattern-moulded sugar bowl of blue flint glass. Stiegel type, 1765–75. The Metropolitan Museum of Art, New York. Gift of F. W. Hunter, 1913.

50 Late seventeenth-century American bottle from New England. American Museum in Britain, Claverton Manor, Bath.

52 A selection of Tiffany 'Favrile' glass.
The Metropolitan Museum of Art,
New York.

53 A pair of Mount Washington faceted candlesticks set with sprays of flowers, and *(Centre)* one of a pair of Whitefriar's opaque-twist millefiori candlesticks. American, nineteenth century. Christie Manson and Woods Limited, London.

53 A pair of Mount Washington faceted candlesticks set with sprays of flowers, and *(Centre)* one of a pair of Whitefriar's opaque-twist millefiori candlesticks. American, nineteenth century. Christie Manson and Woods Limited, London.

profits of an earlier venture, partly by borrowing, was more than just a glass furnace – it was a village community with Stiegel – or Baron Stiegel, as he was respectfully called – very definitely in command. He lived in style with a coach-and-four and a fine house, exercised a paternal control over the education of the children with a bias towards music, and his departures and arrivals were announced by the firing of a cannon. It is sad to read that his energy, ambition and extravagance led to bankruptcy, imprisonment for debt, and death in poverty.

But, unlike most of us, he is still remembered – or was as recently as 1950 – by an unusually charming annual ceremony, the Manheim 'Feast of Roses'. The Lutheran Church paid him a red rose as token rent every year, to the accompaniment of gunfire and band music. The occasion has been revived and a red rose is presented to a descendant.

Whereas it is difficult to identify the Stiegel glass with certainty, there are certain surviving engraved and inscribed glasses which are definitely from Amelung's

45 New Bremen factory in Maryland—all of them in soda-lime metal, although he advertised that he made flint glass; the metal slightly greenish or smoky, the forms characteristically German.

With the gradual opening up of the country during the first half of the nineteenth century the glass industry takes on a new dimension. In the past the chief influence had been German, both in type of metal and in the origin of its people. For many years fine table glass had come from England and Ireland and it was some time before American-made glass was acceptable in fashionable circles. We find the name of Ensell mentioned as early as 1807 in the construction of a glass-house at Pittsburgh—an enterprise which failed for lack of capital. (Once again a descendant of one of the families brought over to England by Carré finds his way across the Atlantic, for Ensell is the English form of Hennezel from Lorraine.) He and his partner, another Englishman, were brought out by two others, Benjamin Bakewell and Benjamin Page, natives of Derby, and it was the Bakewell firm, that survived until 1882, which is considered to have set the standard for future development; from its earliest days this Pittsburgh glass-house was famous for quality. Records are not lacking, but as Pittsburgh became the greatest centre of glass manufacture in the United States, it is difficult to assign individual pieces to any one maker. One of the earliest Bakewell commissions was 'a splendid equipage of glass' ordered by President Monroe in 1817 'consisting of a full set of Decanters, Wine Glasses and Tumblers of various sizes and different models, exhibiting a brilliant specimen of double flint, engraved and cut by Jardelle, in which this able artist has displayed his best manner, and the arms of the United States on each piece have a fine effect'. Another historic event was the presentation to Lafayette, when he visited the plant in 1825, of a pair of vases engraved with the American eagle and a view of the general's home, La Grange.

Success at Pittsburgh in the production of flint glass apparently influenced experiments on the same lines on the Eastern seaboard, until then almost wholly dependent upon importations from England and Ireland. Another circumstance which no doubt had its bearing upon home-grown enterprise was the War of 1812 which, as wars do, put a stop to ordinary business. Again it was an Englishman who began to make the first nineteenth-century flint glass on the East coast, Thomas Cains, a Bristol trained man, who had arrived in Boston in 1811. This was a modest six-pot furnace but was the beginning of great things, for in 1814 some of his workpeople left to set up a furnace in East Cambridge, which was destined to become the New England Glass Company, 47 one of the largest glass establishments in the world.

Cains himself left the Boston plant before 1820 to build a small works of his own near by. This was followed, in 1825, by the foundation of another, scarcely less famous works at Sandwich by Deming Jarves, the first manager of the New England Glass Company. His place at Cambridge was filled by Thomas Leighton, previously a gaffer at Dublin and Edinburgh, who had emigrated with five of his seven sons, all glassmen, a family which remained in charge until 1874. The place was noted for the high lead content of its metal, the simplicity of its forms and careful finish, and also for its colour-work—especially for a ruby formula devised by William Leighton in 1848.

Between 1820 and 1840 at least one hundred glasshouses were in operation, but only in a very few cases is it possible to assign surviving specimens to any one of them. While the enterprises mentioned were building up their well-deserved reputation for high-quality table glass the common or garden houses, making a living chiefly by their coarse bottle glass were also, as a sideline, producing some very distinctive, and sometimes very attractive, bottles and flasks. Less interesting to the world, in general, are numerous pocket flasks reflecting the history of a young country—portraits, for instance of Washington or of Benjamin Franklin, or celebrating the coming of the railroad; of far greater aesthetic value are numerous examples of blown flasks and pocket bottles in brownish glass and other colours, from Ohio and elsewhere.

The important breakthrough was, of course, the invention of the pressing machine, for it was this which made mass production possible and so vastly increased the market. Both Bakewell at Pittsburgh and the New England Glass Company were making knobs in this way 47 by the early 1820s; the first hollow vessel, a salt, was pressed at Cambridge in 1826, while at Sandwich, seventy miles away, Deming Jarves, designed a hand-operated machine which enabled him to produce the first pressed tumbler—an invention which scared his workpeople out of their wits—so much so, that he went in fear of his life and was besieged in his house for six weeks. However, the march of the machine was not to be hindered, the prejudice gradually died down and glassmen, proud of their ancient craft, still found themselves in demand. The epoch-making tumbler was still in existence in 1876 and was exhibited at the Centennial Exhibition, where it was smashed and—surprisingly in view of its historic interest—was not repaired.

For the most part the early pressed wares were flat or shallow objects—plates especially—and a favourite fashion was the so-called lacy glass, that is, pressed glass covered with fine stippling, an effect which could not be obtained by any other method, and often decorated with patriotic and historical subjects, especially on the small cup plates, about three inches in diameter, which were used as cup rests as one drank the tea out of the saucer—a curious sidelight upon the social habits of the day. They are found in all colours, as well as in clear glass, and they seem to have been made wherever this new process was adopted. At the same time simple patterns of fluting in imitation of cut glass were being made in the 1830s—the first pressed goblets for instance. The New England houses remained faithful to flint glass but in the Middle West, by the 1860s, William Leighton had hit upon a soda-lime formula suitable for pressing and a vast amount of cheap wares; a lot of it coloured but of no quality, poured out from dozens of glass factories during

the 70s and 80s. As in Europe, mass production and market expansion produced some deplorable objects—needless to add, not only in glass.

What is remarkable is that in spite of the invention of the pressing process the ancient blowing craft still flourished and the market for elaborate and necessarily expensive pieces did not diminish during the middle years of the nineteenth century. Neither in America nor in Europe could taste be said to be especially distinguished. How could it be when so many of the people with money to spend were so frequently like Dickens's family, the Veneerings, who wanted everything to be shiny and very elaborate and obviously expensive?—tall vases, complicated epergnes, huge chandeliers. There was much wheel-engraving, cutting, and so-called Bohemian ware, the latter imitating the popular imported colour cased glass over clear—all of it handsome in a heavy way, and differing from its Bohemian models by being made of flint glass.

After the Civil War fashion changed, wine glasses were given slender stems instead of solid balusters, and bowls were paper thin. By the 1880s the glassmen were in command of an extraordinary range of technical tricks. They had been making millefiori paperweights, 53 imitating the productions of Baccarat, St Louis and Clichy, as to the manner born, during the 1840s; by the 1880s they had discovered how to produce glass in any colour, or a combination of colours. The best known of these were *Peachblow*, or *wild rose* of the Cambridge works—a name suggested by a Chinese peach bloom porcelain vase which provided a sensation when it fetched a large sum at auction. *Amberina* was another variation (first called *rose amber*), its colour moving from pale amber to rich ruby. Then there was *Burmese*, shading from yellow to coral pink, which so enchanted Queen Victoria that an English house secured the right to manufacture it under licence.

One name, however, must not be omitted, that of 46, 5 Louis Comfort Tiffany (1848–1933) who, greatly influenced in the 1890s by the movement we describe as 'Art 52 Nouveau', did much original experimentation in the chemistry of glass and devoted himself to the manufacture of a series of highly original vessels. He was fascinated by the iridescence of ancient glass after long burial and, in his *Favrile* glass, reproduced it with 46, 5 remarkable fidelity. His forms owe nothing to either Venice or Bohemia but rather to ancient Rome or to Japan and to the natural curving lines, tendrils and trees, of so much French work of his day. A wonderfully interesting searcher after new things; one criticism though seems reasonable—his glass seems to be imitating other metals and is not immediately recognisable as glass.

But all these devices, and many others, did not, on the whole, amount to a great deal, looked at in the light of four thousand and more years of glass history. Perhaps

the developments which have taken place in the
twentieth century are too close to our own time for an
unbiased opinion about them to be possible. An interesting, if fairly brief fashion, catered for by one
enterprising company with some success, decreed that
flower vases, instead of being merely fanciful designs,
should be tailored to the flowers they were intended to
hold—so vases for sweet peas, roses and other blooms
were blown from clear flint glass, or in slightly tinted
green to fit the variously shaped stalks—a sensible and
comely and practical notion which has spread.

Of the more expensive glasses, a firm at Port Jervis,
New York, normally engaged in lighting fixtures,
devised some highly original crackle glass. Much of the
cut decoration of the first half of this century has been of
a very high standard, not plastered over the surface as
was so much of the mid-nineteenth-century work, but
discreetly emphasising the form of the vessel. The most
advanced of all the many concerns which have contri-
buted to what can be described, without exaggeration,
as a renaissance, is the Steuben Glass Company of
Corning, New York, a division of the Corning Glass
Works, which, by a happy chance, did not have to worry
overmuch about finance. The result of the reorganisation
in 1933 was impressive; there was first the establishment
of a flint glass of outstanding quality and next the
designing by talented artists, on the lines of current
Scandinavian practice, of forms and decoration which yet
allow the beautiful metal full play. The results have been
most impressive.

51

Islam

One is not very likely to come across any examples of medieval Islamic glass on the market. Such rarities exist only in fragments, or when undamaged, in museums, a very few private collections and in church and cathedral treasuries – there are, for instance, several in the Treasury of St Marks in Venice, almost certainly loot from the Crusades. Of Museum pieces in England the best known is *The Luck of Edenhall*, a modest beaker in the Victoria and Albert Museum, and a wide, pear-shaped flask in the Slade Collection in the British Museum.

One must, however, mention the most imposing and splendid of all the Islamic glass which has survived the ruinous wars of so many centuries – the fine enamelled lamps of the thirteenth and fourteenth centuries from Egyptian mosques, of which the Victoria and Albert Museum possesses a dozen examples. They are, by the way, always known as lamps, but are, in fact, lampholders; they were suspended from the roof, and a vessel containing oil was placed in them. Both in form and colour they are wonderfully, and at the same time austerely, decorative, often with a text from the Koran to give them religious significance.

Here is one example – 'God is the light of the Heavens and the Earth: His light is as a niche in which is a lamp, the lamp in a glass, the glass as it were a glittering star'. Many of them are also painted with armorials and secular inscriptions which make them into historical documents and also reminders of the mingled squalor, splendour and violence of the thirteenth and fourteenth centuries in Egypt, when a slave might find himself elevated to high office – or even to the Sultanate – at one moment and executed the next. Such an inscription is that on the noble lamp bearing the name of the man known to history as the Sultan Baybars II, who deposed his master temporarily and was master of Egypt for a few months until he was executed in 1310 – a tale of violence and intrigue worthy of the Arabian Nights.

All these lamps are of Syrian workmanship, their inscriptions, beautiful visually, plumbing a depth of obsequiousness typical of all slave states; thus 'Glory to our Lord the Sultan al-Malik al-Muzaffar' – (the victorious King) – 'the Wise the Just, Pillar of the World and the Faith, May his victory be great'. This is followed by a quotation from the Koran – 'Truly the just live in happiness. Thou seest upon their faces the radiance of happiness. They shall have fiery sealed wine to drink'. The other lamp illustrated is remarkable for the Chinese character of its decoration – lotuses and other flowers. The production of these lamps in Syria ended abruptly with the sack of Damascus by Tamerlane in 1400. A few later ones from the fifteenth century are recorded, but mostly of poor quality and one of them in the Arab Museum in Cairo bearing the name of Sultan Qāytbāy is almost certainly Venetian.

In 1480 a man from Milan, named Brascha, visited Jerusalem and noted that vases from Venice were sent to Damascus for one of this Sultan's officials and nearly a century later the Venetian ambassador in Constantinople received an order for lamps to be made in Venice. Obviously the ancient craft based for so long in Syria had fallen upon evil times; considering the violence amid which the glassmen were compelled to work during these centuries, it is astonishing that it survived for so long.

53

Spain

58 Spanish crystal vase and cover with
gold decoration. Royal Factory of La
Granja, 1775-85. Victoria and Albert
Museum, London.

59 Spanish glass water dropper. Catalonia,
seventeenth or eighteenth century.
Victoria and Albert Museum, London.

It is difficult to appreciate the very special atmosphere of Spain and things Spanish until one has spent a little time there off the normal tourist track. Then it gradually comes home to one that this is a country which, in spite of modern communications, is still not quite integrated into Europe. There is a remoteness about its vast plains and the dignified pride and courtesy of its inhabitants which sets the whole nation a little apart from the rest of us and it is not wholly imagination which makes us look south across the Mediterranean and wonder whether the ships on the horizon may not be the advance guard of yet another Islamic invasion. Impossible to forget that the first wave of Muslim invaders landed in 711 and were not finally expelled until after more than seven centuries – and that is a very long time. Some small traces of Islamic conventions can be found in later glass forms, but the invaders were too remote in spirit from the natives to be able to impose their way of life upon them, and, once Ferdinand and Isabella had triumphed at the close of the fifteenth century, Spain became the country we know today, fiercely pious and going its own way.

It is seldom that Spanish glass comes on to the market. An indication of its rarity is provided by the catalogue of the Walter F. Smith Collection which was sent over from Rhode Island to be sold at Sotheby's in 1967 and 1968. Out of 1,032 lots, only seventy-four were of Continental glass. Of these only three were Spanish and even so one of them was by no means a certainty.

In London we are particularly fortunate, for the Victoria and Albert Museum possesses one of the finest collections of Spanish glass in the world, ranging from sixteenth-century pieces from Andalusia to a series of eighteenth-century glasses from the Royal factory of La Granja. Other Spanish glasses are to be seen at the British Museum and in Glasgow. The Hermitage Museum in Leningrad houses about 150, there is an excellent collection in Prague (Museum of Industrial Art), most of it from Catalonia, and there is a further series belonging to the Hispanic Society in New York. Madrid and Barcelona own extensive collections and so does the small town of Peralada, while many of the older Spanish families treasure the glasses which their ancestors acquired directly from their makers.

Spain, of course, as a Roman province, inherited Roman know-how, but little or nothing from those early centuries has survived and the land suffered no less than the rest of Southern Europe from barbarian invasions, not to mention the centuries-long struggle against the Moors. By the end of the fifteenth century documentary evidence begins to throw a little light upon the glass-workers. It seems that by then glass from Barcelona was admired even in Rome itself. There is mention of colours, of blue, purple, tawny yellow and white (that is, uncoloured and transparent) and also a mixture imitating chalcedony.

The earlier documents notice Islamic glass and Catalan imitations in roughly equal numbers, but by about 1450 there is no further mention of imports from the eastern end of the Mediterranean, showing fairly clearly that by now Barcelona was self-sufficient. Some workers from the city set up a glass-house on Mallorca and when, in 1453, the city fathers of Palma drew up a list to combat excessive prices, they noted various shapes as identical with those in fashion on the mainland – decanters, for instance, 'like those of Barcelona' and blown from transparent, colourless glass, high-stemmed glasses, which were no less valuable, and certain vases described as having been made of ordinary glass with a yellowish tint.

By the sixteenth century it was possible to make this claim – 'The glass that today is made in Venice is considered excellent but . . . in many ways, that made in Barcelona and other parts of Cataluña is better . . . and so Cataluña is praised and esteemed for its glass, and boxes are shipped to Castilla, the West Indies; France, Italy, and elsewhere'. One can take all this with several grains of salt, as the very proper pride of a Catalan proud of his native province, but tradition plus the comparatively few authentic specimens which have survived the havoc of the centuries, make it reasonably certain that the claim was not unduly exaggerated.

Throughout the sixteenth and seventeenth centuries Spain was important to the whole of the glass industry in Europe because of the substance known as *barilla*, derived from plants growing in the salt marshes in the neighbourhood of Alicante. It contained soda and a small quantity of lime. It is suggested that the quality of Spanish clear glass in medieval times was due to the use of this substance which was later exported everywhere. An indication of the esteem in which it was held is provided by the report which James Howell sent home in 1621. Howell had been sent abroad by his enterprising boss, Sir Robert Mansell – as tough and shrewd a tycoon as ever existed, with a finger in several pies – to discover what he could about glass manufacture on the Continent. This is what he says:

'I am now . . . come to Alicant[e] the chief Rendezvous I aimed at in Spain, for I am to send hence a Commodity called Barrillia, to Sir Robert Mansel[l], for making of Crystal Glass . . . This Barrillia is a strange kind of Vegetable, and it grows no where upon the Surface of the Earth in that Perfection, as here: . . . It grows thus, It is a round thick earthy Shrub that bears Berries like Barberries, betwixt blue and green; it lies close to the Ground, and when it is ripe they dig it up by the Roots, and put it together in Cocks, where they leave it to dry many Days like Hay; then they make a Pit of a Fathom deep in the Earth, and with an Instrument like one of our Prongs, they take the Tuffs and put fire to them, and when the Flame comes to the Berries, they melt and dissolve into an Azure Liquor, and fall down into the Pit till it be full; then they dam it up, and some Days after they open it and find this Barrillia Juice turned to a blue stone, so hard, that it is scarce malleable; it is sold at one hundred Crowns a Tun . . .'

There is ample documentary evidence to show how lavish were the purchases of both Catalan and Venetian glass by the Royal House and the aristocracy—nor were lesser glass-houses ignored. Thus in 1503 King Ferdinand sent to his Queen Isabella 148 glasses from Barcelona—additions to over 260 pieces already there. We happen to possess details of these glasses, thanks to the industry of a lady-in-waiting who was present when they arrived. It was a very varied consignment—plates, bowls and trays; jugs for water and wine; covered goblets and wine glasses; flower vases and covered jars; wine flasks, salts and cruets; candlesticks and a rose-water sprinkler. There were glasses of several colours, some of them with religious inscriptions, others with writing in Arabic enamelled in colours and white, some gilded or blue or purple or green.

All were part of her bequest to the Royal Chapel at Granada, where the two monarchs lie buried, together with the mad daughter Juana and her French husband. All have long since disappeared, though they were still there in 1526, for the Venetian Ambassador to the Emperor Charles V saw them together with her books, medals and tapestries. It is well known that Charles, the most powerful of monarchs and in absolute command of half Europe, was chronically short of cash; we know he sold Isabella's jewels, and it is quite likely that the other treasures, including the glass, were disposed of at the same time. Governments had not yet learnt the uses of the printing-press in currency problems.

Other documents and inventories show how much admired glasses were from whatever source; they show also, by inference, that the Spanish glass-houses, whether in Barcelona or elsewhere, were able to compete with those of Venice, and, because the fame of Venice was so great, must have been compelled to reach a high standard. In 1560 the third Duke of Albuquerque owned a rare collection, the greater part Venetian, but some from Barcelona and Cadalso. The property of a certain Francisca Ruiz de Castejón in 1586 included glass from Venice and Florence, and also from Barcelona and three other Spanish centres. In 1599 the King's equerry, Diego Fernandez de Cordoba, owned 44 Venetian glasses, many others made in Castile and more than 200 from Barcelona. Earlier still, King Philip II was a lavish purchaser, for the inventory of the contents of the El Pardo palace listed 320 Venetian glasses and 263 from Barcelona; his fourth queen, Anne of Austria, added 300, also from Barcelona. It is noticeable that while the great table services came from Venice and Barcelona, a great deal of the more ordinary domestic glass was brought from Cadalso in

the province of Madrid, a town recorded as early as 1530 as producing far better glass than did other places in the Kingdom of Castile.

As was the case in every European country, all enterprising eyes were turned towards Venice and skilled glassmen, who dared to escape from the harsh yoke of the Serene Republic, were as welcome in Spain as they had been in the Netherlands (at that time part of the Habsburg dominions), in England, in Bohemia and France—though in the case of France the majority of the immigrants came not from Venice, but from Altare. The majority of these Italians remain anonymous, but one of them was Domingo Barovier, a member of one of the best known of the glass families on the island of Murano who, building a furnace at Palma on the island of Mallorca in 1600, advertised that he could manufacture *façon de Venise* 'crystals' (by which he meant clear glass) and that imports were no longer necessary. He seems to have prospered, for eight years later he moved to the mainland and settled in Castile at El Escorial near Philip's grim monastery-palace. Barovier was followed by numerous others from among his countrymen, either direct from Italy or by way of Flanders. Others were Flemish, among them a certain Dieudonné Lambotte who, in 1680, under the patronage of the Spanish governor of the Netherlands, closed down the factory at Namur he had inherited, and moved with his workpeople, and their apparatus, first to Madrid and then near Cadalso.

Throughout the whole of the seventeenth century this influx of skilled people was of considerable benefit to the Spanish industry, but by about 1700 fashion was changing. Instead of the amusing coloured, elaborate confections from Venice, the market began to demand the more substantial engraved vessels of a far clearer, near colourless glass, which was the special contribution of Bohemia and Silesia to European glass-making. This was beyond the abilities of the Spanish houses and, in spite of several attempts with the aid of foreigners to produce something which could compete with the Bohemian 'crystal', success eluded them until, in the mid-eighteenth century, under the patronage of Queen Isabella Farnese, a Catalan, Ventura Sit, was allowed to build a factory in the grounds of La Granja at San Ildefonso. There was a department for the production of mirrors, one for plate glass and a third for lighting fixtures. What concerns us here is that which was devoted to tableware and pieces decorated with engraving, cutting and gilding. Many of the workmen in this section came from France and there was also a highly skilled Swede, Joseph Eder, who was certainly there from 1754 until 1778, perhaps longer. Eder's son, Laurence, was an engraver, trained in the German manner, and there was also a young man from Hanover, Sigismund Brun, who became manager of the shop which specialised in blown crystals and coloured glasses.

60 Spanish glass of the seventeenth
century. Victoria and Albert Museum,
London.

61 Spanish glass with winged handles
showing characteristic Andalusian
proportions. Sixteenth or seventeenth
century. Victoria and Albert Museum,
London.

60 Spanish glass of the seventeenth century. Victoria and Albert Museum, London.

61 Spanish glass with winged handles showing characteristic Andalusian proportions. Sixteenth or seventeenth century. Victoria and Albert Museum, London.

He became manager in 1768 and he was still in charge in 1791.

Although La Granja was never a commercial success and survived only because of royal patronage, its achievements were phenomenal—its metal clear, the taste of its decorators discreet, the ability of its technicians—notably Sigismund Brun—uncommonly high. It was he who discovered a method of firing gilt upon glass, which has stood the test of time remarkably well. The painting was carried out with a brush dipped in a mixture of gold leaf ground up with honey, and the design would be fixed to the surface by firing in a muffle kiln at low temperature and then burnished. There were numerous experiments with coloured and opaque white glass and enamel paints. Coloured glasses include cobalt, emerald and aquamarine, and it was claimed that the milk-white glass was 'produced very perfectly and with it are made various pieces imitating the porcelain of Saxony'.

The archives include the names of several painters who worked both for the San Ildefonso glass-house and also for the Royal Porcelain Factory in Madrid—the famous establishment at Capodimonte near Naples, which Charles III could not bear to leave behind him when he inherited the throne of Spain in 1759 and moved lock, stock and barrel plus its workpeople to Madrid. Fashions —as fashions do—changed again round about 1800 to cut-glass in the English manner. Joseph Bonaparte, made King of Spain in 1808 by his imperious brother, tried to improve its management, condemned the system of royal protection as inefficient and resulting in stagnation, and so 'desirious of opening new ways towards national prosperity' transferred the plant and its Madrid warehouse and shop to private ownership, all creditors to be paid and pensioners to continue to receive their income. It was probably a sensible reform but hardly likely to last in the circumstances of time. When Wellington expelled King Joseph, Ferdinand VII returned to Madrid in 1814 and promptly returned the establishment to the Crown; it remained under royal patronage until 1829, when it was rented to a private company.

57

France

It is curious that a country which, in medieval times, produced such superb stained window glass and, during the last half of the seventeenth and throughout the eighteenth century, was the lode star which drew all eyes to Paris, should have made so small a contribution to Europe's store of really fine table glass. The French themselves, a practical people, realised that something was amiss, for in 1760 the Académie des Sciences offered a prize for suggestions calculated to improve standards, but neither the administrative gifts of Colbert one hundred years previously nor this tardy recognition that all was not well, did much to rejuvenate the numerous glass-houses scattered up and down the land—mostly, of course, in forest areas. It was not until the eighteenth century, when it became absolutely necessary to conserve the vast extent of woodlands, that the trade had to submit to any real form of control, and not until the middle of the nineteenth century that the furnaces of 83 Baccarat and of St Louis produced anything but the most ordinary glasses.

The factory of St Gobain had been established in 1693, but to manufacture mirror glass and so break the monopoly of Venice and to exploit the invention by Bernard Perrot of the casting of plate-glass—a great step forward at the time. Baccarat did not come into operation until 1765, St Louis not until two years later; it can scarcely be argued that either, except at rare intervals, produced anything which could be compared to the current output of their neighbours across the border, or on the other side of the Channel.

Yet there is no lack of evidence that glassmen had been held in high honour from very early times, for in a document dated 1399 Charles VI gives the glass-makers of Mouchamps in Poitou 'the exemptions, freedoms, rights and privileges which the other noblemen in the land use and enjoy and are accustomed to use and enjoy' —no small benefit, for it included valuable tax relief. No less than three times in the same document do we have the assumption that the profession is ancient and noble. The position was succinctly summed up by Garnier in his *History of Glass* of 1886—'In France one remained noble although one was a glassmaker, at Venice one was noble because one was a glassmaker, at Altare one was only a glassmaker because one was a nobleman'. It is an over-simplification, but not very far off target. Garnier omitted one small point in his pithy dictum. In spite of royal decrees, the French glass-maker had to pay for the right to be a gentleman whereas the gentleman born did not.

The evidence for glass tableware as early as the fourteenth century was derived wholly from medieval manuscripts until as recently as 1949, when, during the demolition of a church at Rouen a wine glass was found walled up in a niche. It is now in the Rouen museum proving the accurate observation of the manuscript illustrators for this type of glass—the stem and flower-like bowl (oddly anticipating Art Nouveau mannerisms) are seen on all kinds of tables, high and low, from those of great men down to those of ordinary people.

By about 1450 there were at least 25 glass-houses in operation, and surnames of families destined to make a notable contribution to the industry in England many years later begin to appear in documents, notably three families from Lorraine—Hennezel, Thiétry and Tyzack. Because of their profession they were granted the privileges of noblemen—exemption from taxes, from military service and from having troops billeted among them. They carried swords, wore embroidered hats and became an hereditary caste. One can be reasonably certain that practically all the glass made at this period was forest glass, not to be compared with the finer products of Venice, which became fashionable by the sixteenth century. The result, as with us and in the Netherlands, was a great influx of Italian technicians, in France mostly from Altare, their Italian names speedily Frenchified— Saroldo, for instance, becoming Sarode. In view of the very strong tradition today among the glassmen of Altare, that their ancestors came originally from either France or Flanders, it is interesting to note how, after about 500 years, many of them returned to France and resumed their original French names. It was a migration due partly to the liberal attitude of the Altarist community (so unlike that of the Venetians) and partly to the fortuitous circumstances that the Duke of Nevers, where they first settled, was a relative of the Gonzagas, the lords of Monferrat north of Savona, in which region Altare is situated.

From Nevers Italians spread far and wide. They are recorded at Nantes in 1572 and the place was known in 1588 for its *façon de Venise* glasses; in 1598 others 64 founded a glass-works at St Germain-des-Prés. In 1583 some of them were involved in a dispute with the people of Mâcon, who complained of smoke, of the despoiling of the neighbouring forest, of their exemption from taxes. The townspeople lost. Lyons was another important centre, and there is ample evidence to show that, in the opinion of King and Court, its productions—as those of Nevers and elsewhere—were 'of the same beauty and excellence as those that used to be imported from Venice'. Very, very few glasses which can be attributed to the sixteenth century have survived, and of those most could just as easily have been Venice-made.

By the seventeenth century one can sum up the position by saying that, apart from dozens of small houses turning out rough forest glass, there were four main centres producing the finer kind. Each was protected by a monopoly (a similar system to that used in England). Two were directed by Italians—Nevers and Nantes, two—Paris and Rouen—by French owners employing Italians.

64 Façon de Venise. Probably French, late
sixteenth or early seventeenth century.
Victoria and Albert Museum, London.

65 Candlestick of yellowish glass from the
South of France, eighteenth century.
Musée des Arts Décoratifs, Paris.

By the early years of the seventeenth century, Nevers
63 had become famous for little enamelled glass figures.
There is a record of how Louis XIII, as a child, played
with 'little glass dogs and other animals made at Nevers'
and when, much later in 1622, he visited the town he was
presented with 'a work in enamel representing the
victory His Majesty gained over the rebels of the
pretended reformed religion'. Three years later the town
presented chains and pendant earrings to M. de Nevers,
while his daughter was given chains, earrings and
figures of Our Lady and of St Louis. This type of product
remained in vogue for many years, indeed, until well into
the nineteenth century – both single figures and groups
such as Nativity scenes, the Judgement of Paris and much
else besides. The fact that they were made also in many
other places did not – and still does not – prevent their
being classed as Nevers work. The town became so well
known as the centre for small glass objects of every sort,
that it was known familiarly as 'Little Murano'.

During the first quarter of the eighteenth century,
even the easy-going Government, long aware of the
dangers of deforestation – England had been compelled
to take steps a hundred years previously – began to
enforce some kind of discipline, as a result of which
several glass-houses opened in the neighbourhood of
Caen in Normandy, conveniently situated for coal

imports from England. At the same time, as has already
been noted in the case of Spain, the fashion for Venetian-
type glass was on the wane; everyone who was anyone
demanded the new clear glass from Bohemia, while the
no less new English flint glass, or glass of lead, made very
little headway until quite late in the century. For
instance, we find the royal establishment at St Louis,
hitherto content to manufacture glass *à la façon de
Bohème* since about 1767, began to experiment with the
English formula and, according to the Académie des
Sciences, succeeded in making a French crystal which
was a perfect copy of the English metal. By 1788,
seventy-six workpeople were employed in the production of this so-called crystal and sixty-one in the
production of window-glass, out of a total of three
hundred and sixty.

But not everyone felt that much progress had been
made. Here is a report of 1782 by Macquer:–
'In truth in several French glass-houses clear glasses are
made which are quite fine and to which one gives the
name of crystal, but none of them have either the beauty
or the weight of genuine crystal i.e. that of England, and
in general our French crystal does not enjoy a great
reputation and is not much exported.'

The great contribution which the French made to the
art of glass was yet to come.

England

the eighteenth and nineteenth centuries

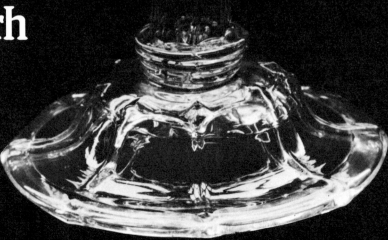

66 English sweetmeat glass on Silesian
stem, *c.* 1725. Victoria and Albert Museum,
London.

67 A famous 'Amen' glass with a Jacobite
inscription. English, mid eighteenth
century. Sotheby and Company, London.

The English contribution to glass technology must not be over-rated; none the less it was considerable and, throughout the whole of the eighteenth century, produced some notable glasses which were as dignified as they were functional. If the reason for making a glass is to provide a comely vessel for wine or any other liquid – one which is not easily broken, which has weight and balance – rather than a pretty, slender, paper-thin confection with a complicated stem and corrugated bowl, then some of the baluster stem goblets of the first half of the century are among the finest to have emerged from a furnace, from so strange and unlikely an amalgam of sand and other ingredients, of which this astonishing material has been composed from beyond man's 29 memory. George Ravenscroft began it and his successors perfected it, so that by about 1700, glass of lead or flint glass, as it was called indiscriminately, became standard throughout the country.

Until 1745, glass was not subject to a tax: in that year an excise tax was levied – a tax calculated by weight – and it was this as much as other considerations (inevitable change of fashion, the search for fresh ideas and so forth) which led glassmen to devise more slender glasses and to attract business by pretty tricks with colour twists. The early types of glasses are generally baluster stems in one form or another, with a fashion for the so-called Silesian stem (which has, in fact, nothing to do with Silesia) – high-shouldered and fluted – in favour for perhaps twenty or so years after George I came to the throne in 1714, and – another admirable shape – the drawn stem glass, a type in which the stem is not made separately, as it is with the others, but is drawn from the trumpet-shaped bowl in one operation. Both types, baluster and drawn stem, frequently contain an air-bubble or tear which can be, and was, developed into an airtwist, advertised as early as 1737 as 'wormed glasses' or 'wrought glasses'.

It is these drawn stem glasses which were, on rare occasions, embellished with diamond-point engraving of the royal crown and cypher and the Jacobite national anthem. Perhaps one verse will suffice:

'God save the Church I pray,
And bliss the Church I pray,
Pure to remain,
Against all Heresie
And Whigs' Hypocrisie
Who strive maliciously
Her to defame.'

Such things are great rarities, nostalgic memories of long past loyalties and tragedies, hopes which were finally dissipated by the Battle of Culloden in 1746. Other Jacobite glasses were made for about twenty years after the disaster – not very choice aesthetically and, on 67 the whole, rather clumsily engraved with the emblems of the various Jacobite societies—the rose with two buds (the Old Pretender and his two sons) sometimes, but rarely, a portrait of Prince Charles Edward—and the inevitable counter from the Hanoverian Establishment, Williamite glasses, engraved no less clumsily with an

88 equestrian portrait of William III.

In the seventeenth century, rough bottle glass was good enough to be used for what we now call a decanter, and the earliest decanters—if one can call them that—began to be made in clear glass; a type of perhaps the 1730s has just the bulbous shape of the early bottle and, moreover, has a projecting rim for tying on a cork with string. But by the mid-eighteenth century, glass stoppers have become normal. At first decanters are club-shaped with pointed stoppers, then they become more slender with flat stoppers in the form of vertical discs. By 1800 stoppers are mushroom-shaped, mostly it seemed made in Ireland where, until 1825, no excise existed to prevent the use of heavy metal.

Simple and very charming engraving—grapes and vine leaves on wine glasses, hops and barley on ale glasses—was popular from about the mid-1730s to the 1760s. Enamelling was not in favour in England until the 1760s, when it was used in two ways. The first was in

98 Newcastle, where members of the Beilby family, only rarely using colours, devised a highly original type of decoration by painting the clear glass with birds, or vine leaves, or ruins, in opaque white. The second was painting on opaque white glass obviously imitating

21 Chinese porcelain models; this opaque white was formerly attributed almost wholly to Bristol, but it was certainly produced in many other centres.

The two great achievements of the English glassmen of the last half of the eighteenth century were first the variety of colour twists in the stems of wine glasses and secondly—and far more important—the development of cutting, a technique already practised to some extent by the 1740s. The Excise Act of 1745 and others of 1777, 1781 and 1787, certainly encouraged the trade to think hard about means of producing lighter glasses and to invent decorative details. Fortunately, the English formula had produced a glass beautifully adapted for cutting because of its light-dispersing quality.

The familiar four-sided bottles for spirits with cut decoration seem to have been in favour by the mid-eighteenth century, and the advantage given to Ireland by the absence of an excise duty was largely responsible for the development of Irish glass-making from about 1780. The English maker was thus guided towards slender forms; the Irish furnaces—managed, it should be said, by English technical men—towards the deep cutting which was in fashion for the next half century. The Irish were not subject to any excise duty until 1825. The English were hampered in this way until 1845.

The 1820s, in Europe as in America, witnessed the

emergence of a vast new middle class with money in its pockets, and the beginnings of mechanisation. Taste ran to cased or flashed glass in ruby, blue and in opaque white, just as it did in Bohemia, where the industry was experiencing a revival. On the whole, there is very little to be said for the more pretentious glass of the period (see the catalogue of the Great Exhibition of 1851 for some singular monstrosities) but much praise is due to the dark brownish-green jugs and bottles from Nailsea, with their variegated colour splashes. The American invention

of pressed glass began to influence the English glass-makers in the 1830s and was, and still is, used to reproduce, however roughly, the appearance of cut glass – but it can be no more than a cheap substitute.

It was John Ruskin who, in *The Stones of Venice* (1851–3), sowed a seed which was to bear fruit years later. He denounced cut glass as being against the nature of the material and admired only vessels which owed their form to the manipulation of the metal. He over-stated his case, but his opinion carried weight. The theories of William Morris also influenced design so that, in one way and another, particularly in the work carried out over many years by the Whitefriars Glass-works (James Powell and Sons), the early tradition of hand-made blown glass was recovered again. By comparison, the cameo glass in imitation of the Portland Vase, technically accomplished and necessarily extremely expensive, which was made at Stourbridge by John Northwood and the brothers Woodall, seems uncom-monly insipid and sugary.

68

70, 78

Modern
Times

69 A pair of vases by Thomas Webb and
Sons. Queen's Burmese ware. English,
c. 1887. Private Collection.

All countries, and not England alone, were subject to the
unrelenting march of the Machine Age with the con-
sequent emergence of a new public, and a puzzled
acceptance of what we now consider uncommonly bad
taste. The novels of Dickens, and to an even greater
degree those of Balzac, depict for us this oddly confused
society which was at the same time vigorous, brash and
so often unsure of itself. Certainly the glass industry in
Europe managed to produce quite singular horrors and
some of the finest glass objects known to man, as well as
a legion of sensible, down-to-earth domestic glass which
added enormously to the amenities of life.

A minor phenomenon of the period, after the
Napoleonic wars, was the new-found freedom of travel,
with the result that some endearing glass tourist
souvenirs were concocted, the best of them engraved
portraits and landscapes by Dominik Biemann (1800–57)
who worked mainly in Prague, but moved to Franzensbad
during the holiday season. Another gifted engraver was
August Böhm (1812–90) who wandered over Europe
and visited England and America. Side by side with all
this activity, on a small scale, the Bohemian industry
embarked upon colour in a big way – a reaction against
the eighteenth-century vogue for clear crystal – ruby-
red, tones of green, blue and amethyst, greenish-yellow,
yellowish-green, antimony, topaz and amber. There was
a dense black opaque glass registered as Hyalith, and a
marble glass known as Lithyalin. Far superior to all these
experiments has been the work carried out for a century
and more by the firm of J. & L. Lobmeyr of Vienna, with
furnaces both in Austria and in what was once Bohemia –
including intaglio and linear engraving, cutting and
enamel painting in the modern manner.

In the world of glass, France can be said to have come
of age by the 1850s, not by way of the ingenious glass
paperweights which have been such market darlings
for so long, but because of the high quality of the metal
in the normal output of the furnaces of Baccarat and 83
elsewhere, at first in the fashion of the day – cut or
engraved glass, either crystal, coloured, flashed or
stained silver-yellow – and in our own times with the
emphasis upon harmony of form, instead of elaborate
decoration. But much of this was run-of-the-mill stuff.

It was not until the latter part of the century that an
outstanding designer placed France firmly on the map.
This was Emile Gallé (1846–1904) who, as I have written 71
elsewhere on several occasions, 'whether as theorist,
designer, practical glass man or successful man of
business, is the dominating figure of the last years of the
19th century'. Gallé's father owned a well-established
faïence and furniture business at Nancy, while his
mother inherited a mirror factory. With this solid
financial background he was in a position to experiment
and the result of his experiments were first seen in the
year 1878 when, at the Paris Exhibition, his enamelled

70 Translucent red cameo glass plaque by George Woodall. English, c. 1890.

71 Bottle by Emile Gallé after a design by Victor Prouvé. The base is inscribed: 'Emile Gallé Nancy, Exposition 1889'.

70   71

72 Solomon and the Queen of Sheba.
Swedish glass by Simon Gate which was
shown at the Paris Exhibition of 1925.
Orrefors Glassworks, Sweden.

72

73 Glass inkwell by the Daum brothers, the lid formed of a conventionalised anemone with yellowish cream opaque glass; the base engraved with foliage. French, late nineteenth century. By courtesy of Mrs Joan Collins.

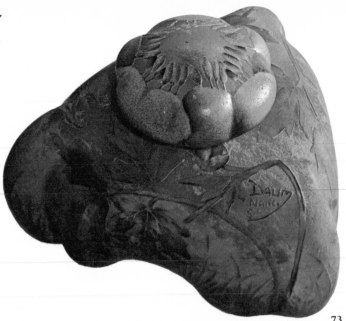

73   74

75

glass with gold leaf inserted between the layers, and his opaque, coloured and marbled glass, made his name.

His great triumph came five years later, when the style which will always be associated with him was seen for the first time—a highly poetic manner based upon his delight in flowers and trees and gardens, not founded upon book learning, but upon his own observation as gardener and botanist. All this idealism he translated into terms of glass—'My personal work consists of dreaming up tender and dramatic roles for crystal. As far as I can, I impose in advance on this flowing and varied material the qualities which I consider it possesses—its colours, its form—to bring to life my dream, my design'. He was perhaps fortunate to have lived just when he did. His work was very personal

and too subtle and delicate for his many followers wholly to assimilate. He, more than anyone, raised the standards of the French glass industry and achieved world-wide renown.

His influence was felt as far afield as Norway and New York, where Louis Comfort Tiffany (1848–1933) 46, 51 who had several interests besides glass became as well 52 known as Gallé himself. His neighbours in Nancy, the brothers Daum, learned much from him and began to 73 make flower-decorated glasses in his manner in 1890. He and his followers are inevitably bound up in the movement we know as 'Art Nouveau'. He is sometimes referred to as its chief inventor; that is not so, but he was one of its most distinguished exponents.

The First World War changed all that. The flowing,

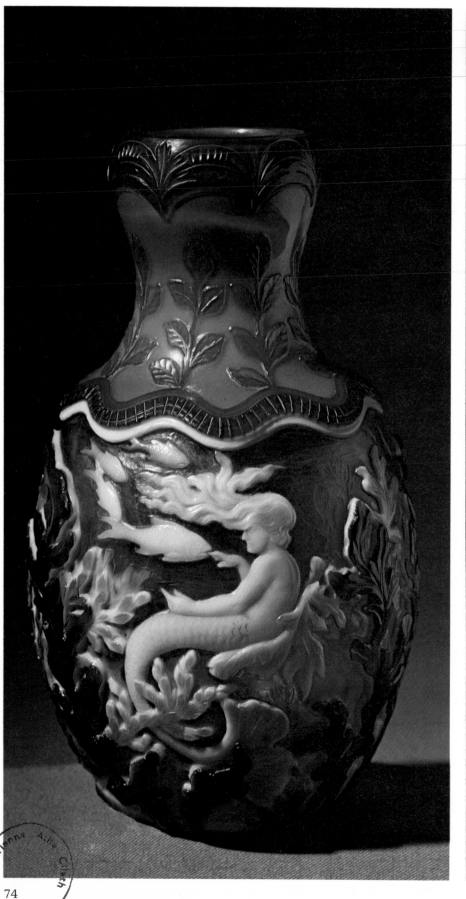

Three diverse glasses of no great consequence.
(Left to Right) Square spirit bottle decorated in
gilt. Perhaps Liège, early nineteenth century.
Modern Spanish vase, bought a few years ago
for 10s. Bohemian engraved cup, mid nineteenth
century. By courtesy of the author.

80 Stipple-engraved glass by Laurence
Whistler (b. 1912), inspired by Castle
Howard Mausoleum. Victoria and Albert
Museum, London.

THE MAUSOLEUM

81 Glass engraved by John Hutton
(b. 1906), who gave a new impetus to this
craft in recent years by his engraving on
the doors of Coventry Cathedral. By
courtesy of the author.

82 Late Victorian cranberry glass basket; 83 A pair of modern Baccarat candlesticks.
retail price: £10. Private Collection. By courtesy of the author.

82 Late Victorian cranberry glass basket; retail price: £10. Private Collection.

83 A pair of modern Baccarat candlesticks. By courtesy of the author.

84 Decanter with gilt decoration. Perhaps Liège, early nineteenth century. Bought by the author, ten or fifteen years ago, in a junk shop in Lincolnshire for 5s. By courtesy of the author.

85 Green-tinted, 'soap-bubble design' vase
by Kaj Franck. Finnish, 1955. Victoria and
Albert Museum, London.

plant-like curves of the recent past were now rather old hat; so was elaborate ornamentation, so was–to a limited extent–colour. Of two notable French technicians who must not be forgotten, one is Maurice Marinot (1882–1960), friend of Matisse and Derain, who became fascinated by glass and so deserted painting. His work is limited, very rare and highly personal. The second, René Lalique (1860–1945), made his name as a designer of Art Nouveau jewellery. A commission from Coty for perfume bottles set him upon a course which, between the wars, enabled him to impose his ideals upon the world of fashion–mostly colourless glass with a frosted surface, ice-cool formal patterns described by enthusiasts as having 'the etherial brilliance of Arctic ice'. (A typical overstatement).

In the twentieth century, the northern countries of Europe, Sweden in particular, suddenly come to the fore with highly original work, most of it beautifully simplified table glass–clean lines, no fussy ornamentation–in accordance with the austere theories of the day. But the Swedes had taken industrial design seriously for many years; their Society of Industrial Design was founded as long ago as 1845. An innovation was the slogan 'Let the Artist design for Industry'. Two men, both painters, Simon Gate and Edward Hald, were engaged by a modest glass-house at Orrefors (founded 1898), which soon became famous first for its Graal glass, an offshoot of the Gallé manner, and secondly for its engraving, which had a great success at the Paris Exhibition of 1925. Other Swedish and Scandinavian glass-houses followed the example of Orrefors in engaging artists from outside the industry with the happiest results.

Italy, until after the First World War, remained strangely behind the times, producing many pretty glasses in the manner of its distant and distinguished past, but apparently unaware that time was marching on. Two exceptional men among many admirable technicians brought Venice back to something like its early reputation for bold experiments. The first is Paolo Venini from near Milan who, in 1921, with the Venetian Giacomo Cappelin, established a glass-house in the traditional home of the craft, Murano. At first, he made glasses adapted from those familiar from early paintings, both colourless and tinted. Later, he experimented with various colours and textures, among them an opaque glass containing numerous air-bubbles, another type treated with acid to give it a rough, apparently corroded surface, and a third–a bubbly glass encased in a transparent layer–has simple forms and colour and texture varied.

The second is Ercole Barovier, an honoured name in glass-making history, for the family can be traced back to the fifteenth century. He has been responsible for

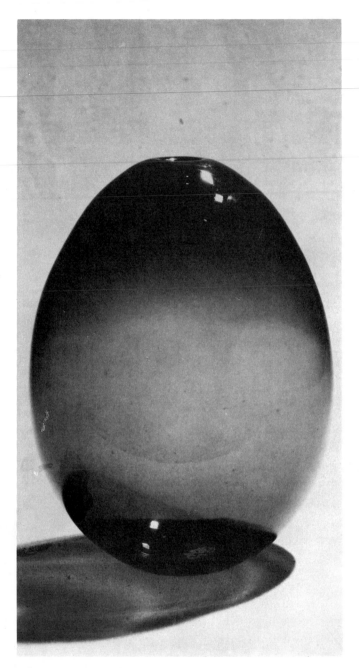

many permutations and combinations–from 'lizard' glass (a mottled green) to a coloured mosaic dusted with gold.

The story of glass is already four thousand years old and is far from ended, for the material is so ductile and amenable, that he must be a dull dog indeed who can imagine that human ingenuity (aided by the rare genius) will not devise other and perhaps yet more delectable and useful forms and methods of decorating them. Meanwhile let twentieth-century man be grateful to the anonymous thousands of toilers who have left him so astonishing an inheritance.

86 Vase by Venini. Venice, twentieth
century. Victoria and Albert Museum,
London.

87 Vase by Ercole Barovier. Streaked
decoration under an outer casing of clear
glass outside, and powdered gold inside.
Murano, 1951. Victoria and Albert Museum,
London.

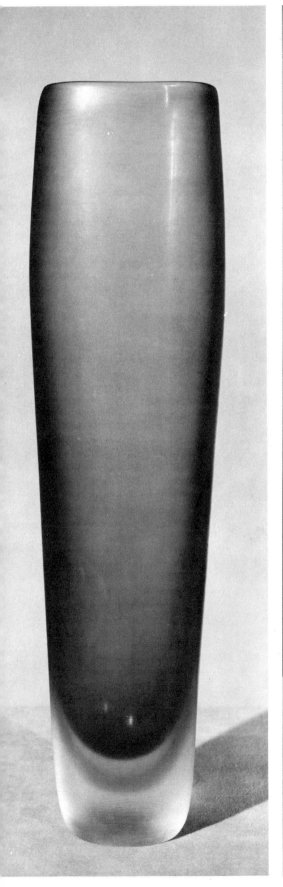

Money

All who read this book will probably take some interest in costs, even if they have no particular desire to become serious collectors. He would be a bold man who would venture to prophesy what is likely to happen to prices in the future. If the value of money continues to fall, it is reasonable to suppose that prices will rise. Moreover, the supply of interesting and worthwhile glasses is not unlimited. The better ones gradually find their way into museums and so are permanently removed out of reach, leaving lesser rarities with a great scarcity value.

On the other hand, collecting fashions can change, and what was popular in one decade can become unsaleable in the next. In short, there is no hard and fast rule one can lay down as a guide to ensure that the collector of today, however careful and however earnest in the pursuit of knowledge, never loses any money. Indeed, if everything on the financial side was cut and dried, half the fun would be drained out of a pursuit which can be as innocent as it is absorbing.

A collector who expects to make a profit on everything he buys is, I suggest, a fool. If, after a lapse of time, he discovers that what he has bought has appreciated in value, he has every reason to rejoice. But if the contrary happens, he should remember that the purchase of a fine glass can be at least as great a pleasure as a week-end by the sea, or in Paris in agreeable company. When he returns from such a trip he does not expect to get his money back. In the same way he should buy works of art because he wants to live with them and enjoy them, and if he has chosen wisely, he will be able to make two profits—the first and the most important and one which cannot be reckoned in terms of cash, namely the delight of having a nice thing to live with, the second, if he must sell, a reasonably handsome dividend on his original investment. If he loses, so what?—he has had his holiday.

Few of us, though, have unlimited money; few of us are so pig-headed that we buy something without taking pains to discover whether the price we are asked bears some relation to the prices paid for similar objects elsewhere. If the glass which has taken our fancy turns out to be unique (in the literal sense of a word which is so often used very loosely) we must not be surprised if we have to pay over £1000 for it. But such things are exceptional. Most good glasses from the past—even from the distant past—whether from the Roman world or from our own of the eighteenth and nineteenth centuries are to be had for well under £50 each. This is a statement of fact which will perhaps do something to calm the fears of the neophyte, who reads from time to time of some great rarity fetching £2,000 to £3,000 at auction and is liable to be frightened away from a market which he has not yet had time to explore.

I consider that a wise newcomer, after roaming round for a time getting his bearings, will make friends with one or other of the half dozen first class dealers who

specialise in this most delectable of metals. Let him sit at their feet for a time, listen carefully, and generally, if not always, take their advice. He will find them both erudite and shrewd. He will also—that goes without saying—make himself familiar with the history of glass manufacture, accustom his eyes to the various shapes in favour from time to time in many countries, and put his memory to the test by looking carefully at the superb collections in, to mention only two which are readily accessible in London, the British Museum and the Victoria and Albert Museum, or the Corning Museum of Glass in New York. Let him look hard and form his own opinion before reading any explanatory matter. He will probably realise the extent of his ignorance; let him not despair but remember that ignorance is the beginning of knowledge. By this means he will acquire humility and the capacity to laugh at himself.

What follows is a purely factual account of the prices paid in the early part of 1972 at three sales in London which can be described as good, average specialist dispersals of early glass. I should emphasise that these prices were either actually paid at these three auctions or, in perhaps about ten per cent of the lots, were the prices at which they were bought in.

It is necessary to point our that no one in his senses expects a dealer to let him have a glass for the same sum the glass has fetched at auction. It should not be necessary to say this, but I have known instances in which a would-be purchaser has been annoyed with a dealer because the latter has demanded what the former considered an excessive profit. The dealer puts his knowledge and reputation against an unfeeling world; the client has no valid complaint if the dealer demands, say, 100 per cent profit. The dealer has the perfect answer—'I was prepared to pay £200 for this glass and it fell to me at £100. If you had bid against me I should have run you up to my limit, £200. Why didn't you?' He is perfectly justified, but it is extraordinary how cross some people become when faced by this kind of situation.

As to what is a fair price, that is anybody's guess. Perhaps not a bad method, after due consideration, is to ask yourself these two questions: 1. Do you like it? Yes. 2. Can you afford it? Yes. Why then all this fuss?

First sale SOTHEBY'S JANUARY 24TH, 1972
This first sale analysed here, English and Continental Glass, 234 lots, which realised £12,003 ($29,400) or—to the nearest £ sterling—an average of a trifle over £50($122) per lot.

On this occasion the highest price was the £500 ($1,225) given by the National Museum of Dublin for a rare
88 Williamite wine glass, a decidedly clumsy glass, its stem far too thick for elegance. This was a typical instance in which historical associations far outweigh other criteria, for the glass was engraved with a mounted King William

III beneath a ribbon inscribed: *The Glorious Memory of King William III*—in short, an example of naïve pro-Establishment propaganda in opposition to the many glasses in circulation after the 1715 rebellion, engraved with inscriptions and emblems (a rose with two buds etc.) symbolising the cause of the Old Pretender. The trumpet bowl is well enough, but few will be found to pretend that the cylinder stem is a masterpiece of craftsmanship. Its value then was due almost wholly to the loyal engraving.

Compare this with the glasses on each side—nice things; indeed, a cut above the average, but in no way extraordinary, yet far easier to live with. The one on the left, 88 to be dated perhaps to about 1760, is a type characteristic of the work of a little glass factory at Lynn in Norfolk—a round funnel bowl with typical horizontal moulding (impossible to reproduce this detail in a photograph), the stem composed of a double series of opaque twists, the foot conical. It made £50($122).

A glass with an ogee bowl with thick sides and very 89 deceptive, the stem beneath a shoulder knop containing a tear (only just visible in the photograph), conical foot, went for £80 ($196). Here at least is one lesson well and truly demonstrated—that aesthetics have little to do with market values.

Four other glasses found new owners at between £250($612) and £300($735). The three hundred pounder —not considered worth an illustration in the catalogue— was a fine 7¼in. (18.5cm.) high baluster-stem wine glass, with a straight-sided bowl with solid base on a bold acorn knop above a base knop with a continuous tear.

The two hundred and eighty pounder was a well- 90 mannered covered goblet, with a fluted high-shouldered so-called Silesian stem, engraved with a seated woman holding a cornucopia—the stem and cover finial star-studded, 10½in. (26·8cm.) high.

The early rummer next to it—the name derived from 90 the German *Roemer*, so familiar with its raspberry prunts applied round the stem—has a frilled collar, a hollow cylindrical stem and trailed decoration above gadrooning on the lower half of the bowl, must be pre-1700 and is considered as perhaps from the glass-house of Hawley Bishop, c. 1685. It fetched £260 ($637).

A great many people are likely to find that of all the many varieties of English wine glasses, those whose stems contain twists, whether opaque white or multi-coloured, are the most attractive. The fairly simple type is seen in the glass from the Lynn factory already noticed. A far more complicated stem is shown in the bell bowl, 91 supported on a double-knopped stem enclosing six spirals in tones of blue, mauve, white and yellow—a considerable rarity which fetched £250 ($612). Next to 91 it is a second rarity, a glass with a bell bowl supported on a double-knopped multi-spiral air twist. This made £190 ($466).

90 *(Left)* A rummer, perhaps from the glass-
house of Hawley Bishop, *c.* 1685, which fetched
£260 ($637). *(Right)* A covered goblet with
Silesian stem, engraved with a seated woman
holding a cornucopia, which fetched £280 ($686).
Both auctioned at Sotheby and Company, London.

91 *(Left)* A glass with a bell bowl supported on a double-knopped multi-spiral air-twist. This made £190 ($466). *(Centre)* A bell bowl supported on a double-knopped stem enclosing six spirals in tones of blue, mauve, white and yellow, which fetched £250 ($612). *(Right)* A glass with an upright columnar stem decorated with an incised twist. It was sold for £40 ($98). All auctioned at Sotheby and Company, London.

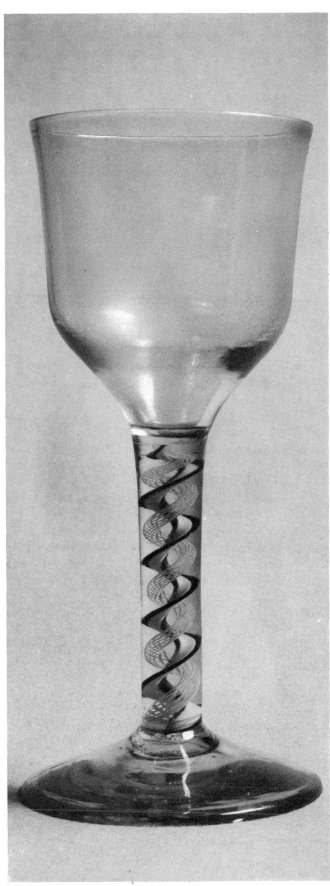

92 A plain ogee-bowl glass supported on an opaque white spiral cable, encircled by a white corkscrew ribbon edged with translucent orange and green. This fetched £1,000 ($2,450) at a sale on the 10th of April, 1972, at Sotheby and Company, London.

On the other hand, a glass which does not conform to any of the standard, well-recognised types, however unusual and delectable it may be, does not attract nearly so much attention—as witness the undoubted charmer on the right of these two twist rarities. Its round funnel bowl is moulded to within ¼in. (7mm) of the rim, the upright columnar stem decorated with an incised twist. It was sold for £40 ($98).

Of the remaining lots, 16 fetched between £100 ($245) and £200 ($490) while the rest, 159 in number, went for below £50 a piece. Included among these also-rans, as always in a sale of this character, were various lots of from 4 to 12 glasses; 12 sherry glasses, plus a spare of a slightly different type, for instance, which were bought for £25 ($61); a pair of small decanters and stoppers (nineteenth-century cut glass) made £7 ($17); 6 thistle-shaped tumblers, also cut glass, £28 ($69).

Second sale SOTHEBY'S APRIL 10TH, 1972
This was a smaller dispersal than the previous one, but it happened to include a greater proportion of unusual lots, so that the average price was very much higher—£90 ($220) as compared with £51 ($125).

The highest price was £1,000 ($2,450) given for a very beautiful ogee bowl glass supported on an opaque white spiral cable encircled by a white corkscrew ribbon edged with translucent orange and green. This had appeared in the same rooms on three previous occasions during the preceeding 20 years. In 1952 (Applethwaite-Abbot Collection) it had been sold for £56 ($137); in 1960 (Sir Hugh Dawson) for £160 ($392); in 1967 (Smith Collection) for £420 ($1,029). The unusual combination of colours, no doubt, mainly accounted for a four-figure price.

£570 ($1,396) was given for a late seventeenth-century 'crizzled' goblet, its bucket bowl 'nipt-diamond waies' on the underside, supported on a tall stem composed of two hollow-blown quatrefoil knops. This had been in the Horridge sale in 1959, and in the Smith Collection in the 1968 dispersal made £320 ($784).

Two other late seventeenth-century glasses realised nearly as much. One of them was an ale glass in the manner of Venice, its funnel bowl vertically ribbed and pincered, resting on a single collar above a winged stem. This was seen at Sotheby's as long ago as 1929 in the Kirkby Mason Collection, it reappeared in 1956 (£80–$196) and again in the Smith Collection 1968 (£520–$1,274). It now made £500 ($1,225).

The other was an early goblet supported on a bobbin stem of eight knops, its wide conical foot unevenly folded round the rim. This also had been seen previously, first in the Savile Collection in 1919 when it sold for £38 ($93); in an anonymous sale in 1956 it was sold for £55 ($135), and in the Smith Collection for £470 ($1,151). It now made £440 ($1,078).

88

glasses, each with a trumpet bowl engraved with a border of trellis work and doves. The set fetched £310 ($759). Both auctioned at Sotheby and Company, London.

96-97 Early nineteenth-century Bohemian glass. *(Left)* Octagonal beaker, enamelled in ochre and decorated in gilt and silver with lyres. This fetched 28 guineas ($71). *(Right)* Hexagonal beaker, enamelled in colours and gilt, with a monkey, birds and insects among flowers and scrolling foliage. This fetched 55 guineas ($142). Both auctioned at Christie Manson and Woods Limited, London.

94

95

96   97

98 *(Left)* A Newcastle glass enamelled in white in the workshop of the Beilby family, one side decorated with a peacock, the reverse with the inscription JNo and M. Harrison and the date 1768. This beaker was bought for 250 guineas ($642).

(Centre) Two sweetmeat glasses—the one on the left, with its straight column stem, made 60 guineas ($154); the one on the right, with an indented stem, made 85 guineas ($220). *(Right)* A glass with its bowl gadrooned and its stem with a

cushion knop above a hollow dumb-bell section—a shape always catalogued as a mead-glass—which went for 140 guineas ($360). All auctioned at Christie Manson and Woods Limited, London.

There were four between £300 ($735) and £400 ($980). One of them was sold for £380 ($931), as well-balanced, as solid an English glass as one could wish for, with an unusual stem–round funnel bowl with solid base, then an acorn knop and a base knop on a folded conical foot.

Another made £320 ($784)–an armorial goblet, a typical example of a Newcastle glass engraved in Holland with the arms of the Province of Friesland, the round funnel bowl slightly flared.

A third, which made £360 ($882), was a goblet and cover, engraved with the head of Britannia and the inscription *O Fair Britannia Hail* amid a design of acorns, hops and barley, flowers on the domed cover and the foot, the base of the bowl faceted as also the knop on the cover, the stem cut with small diamonds.

A fourth lot which perhaps is not quite a fair comparison, because it was one of a set of 4 sold as one lot, made £310 ($759). One of the set of 4 is illustrated here–a very pretty set–typical Newcastle slender baluster types, each with a trumpet bowl engraved with a border of trelliswork and doves.

Of the remaining glasses, 13 realised between £200 ($490) and £300 ($735); 24 between £100 ($245) and £200 ($490), while 86 were sold for less than £50 ($122) each. Among glasses which fetched less than £100, a more than normally attractive and certainly rare finger bowl, presumably eighteenth-century, blue in colour, the bowl moulded with graduating horizontal rings, a type generally attributed to the factory at Lynn–a simple shape anticipating the twentieth century–fetched £75 ($184).

Someone acquired a nice pear-shaped Venetian vase for £5 ($12), someone else a pair of nineteenth-century decanters and stoppers–coarsely cut I admit–for £4 ($10), and a third person four pretty scent bottles complete with stoppers for £10 ($25). Stoppers, by the way, on odds and ends such as scent bottles and on decanters, are frequently missing; replacements are normal.

Third sale CHRISTIE'S APRIL 25TH, 1972
On this occasion there were 323 lots, the total reached £14,031 ($34,376)–average price £43 ($105). The highest price, 480 guineas ($1,235), was offered for an amusing set of 4 figures of the Seasons from Nevers in France, the town which specialised in these pretty and vulnerable tourist attractions.

A single wine bottle of 1764 bearing the seal of All Souls College, Oxford, made 30 guineas ($79), a single bottle without a seal one guinea, 48 wine bottles impressed with the crest of Sir John Carew-Pole, Bart., averaged 3½ guineas ($10) each.

One lot was composed of four whimsies of Nailsea glass, three of them walking sticks, one a trumpet. One of the walking-sticks was pale turquoise with spiral

fluting, the trumpet clear glass with spirally moulded flutes–all four amusing, splendidly useless objects which were sold together for 20 guineas ($52).

A pair of ship's decanters and stoppers–the sensible shape, wide in the base, tapering to a narrow neck to avoid disaster when the stormy winds do blow–are always in demand and fetched 48 guineas ($122) while, among a series of cut glass pieces, a pair of candlesticks, their vase-shaped stems faceted and with a band of diamond-cutting and with faceted drops suspended from nozzles and star-shaped canopies above, fetched 70 guineas ($181).

Among rather rarer glasses was a Newcastle glass enamelled in white in the workshop of the Beilby family, one side decorated with a peacock, the reverse with the inscription JNo and M. Harrison and the date 1768. An inscription and date inevitably raises the price, and this beaker was bought for 250 guineas ($642). Two sweetmeat glasses–the first with its straight column stem made 60 guineas ($154), the other, with an indented stem, made 85 guineas ($220). Each was early, with a gadrooned bowl. A glass with its bowl also gadrooned, its stem with a cushion knop above a hollow dumb-bell section, a shape always catalogued as a mead glass (I

suspect for a wholly insufficient reason), went for 140 guineas ($360).

The final half hour or so that morning was occupied by the dispersal of a series of early nineteenth-century Bohemian glasses in various colours and shapes, some of them technically highly accomplished, if lacking in the easy elegance of their ancestors. Two beakers were a **96** fair sample. One was octagonal, enamelled in ochre and decorated in gilt and silver with lyres. This fetched **97** 28 guineas ($71), and one went for 55 guineas ($142). It was also hexagonal, enamelled in colours and gilt with a monkey, birds and insects among flowers and scrolling foliage.

Finally, to conclude this purely factual discussion on market values—values which do not by any means always bear any relationship to aesthetic values—here are two examples, each of them admirable in their own way, as unlike one another as cricket and rugby, and with as great a contrast in price as can be imagined.

The first, is a noble goblet, 8½in. (21·6cm.) high, about **99** as fine a glass decorated by William Beilby of Newcastle as exists. It is well known, first seen in public at the *Exhibition of Art Treasures* at the Grafton Galleries in May 1928, at the Victoria and Albert Museum (*The Circle*

of Glass Collectors Commemorative Exhibition) in 1962 and at Manchester in 1964. It was clearly a special commission, and as it was a heraldic piece, Beilby was necessarily bound to use colour in addition to his normal opaque white enamel. The deep bucket bowl is enamelled in tones of green, buff, red and white with the arms of the Couper family impaling Gray within a characteristic Rococo gilt border, the reverse with the family crest between two white butterflies. There are traces of gilding on the rim, the foot is conical, and the stem encloses a double series of opaque twist spirals. In the Horridge Collection in 1959 it fetched £1,120 ($2,744). At Sotheby's, early in 1972, it was bought for £3,100 ($7,595).

The second is an exceedingly elegant, nineteenth- **84** century vessel, which is possibly from the neighbourhood of Liège. It is—at the moment at any rate—wholly unfashionable, but gives me enormous pleasure whenever I catch sight of it. Ten or fifteen years ago I went into a junk shop in Louth in the hope of finding a painting fit to live with. There was no such thing, but this decanter was in the window. I asked the price and was told—'Oh that rubbishy thing!—five shillings'. I did not haggle.

Trade Jargon

Agate glass General term for glass of several colours mingled before shaping to imitate semi-precious stones–chalcedony, jasper, onyx and agate

Air twist Wine glass stems made by elongating and twisting a lump of glass containing one or more air bubbles

Barilla The soda-charged ash of sea plants exported from Spain

Batch The weighed and mixed ingredients (sand, soda etc.) placed in the fire-clay pot or crucible for melting

Bottle glass The common term for ordinary glass with a greenish or brownish tone which has not been decolourised

Cameo glass Usual name for the technique by which an outer layer of white was carved against a coloured background. The most famous example is the Portland Vase

Colour twist stems Opaque white and coloured threads of glass manipulated in the same manner as air twist stems, often combined with the latter. Popular during the 1750s and 60s

Crizzling A network of interior cracks due to an excess of alkali in the mixture. A defect mostly found in seventeenth-century glass made in England, Germany, the Netherlands and China. The defect was cured in Germany by adding lime in the form of chalk, in England by oxide of lead

Cullet Broken glass. Waste from the glass-houses mixed in the batch. Cullet was never left lying about, but, unlike broken pottery or porcelain, could be used again

Diamond engraving Scratching a design with a diamond

Firing glass Squat glass with short stem and thick foot to stand up to hammering on the table at drinking parties. A similar glass but thickened in the bowl to diminish its capacity was provided for the toastmaster

Gaffer The skilled craftsman who manipulates the molten glass. He sits in a chair which has long, flat parallel arms on which the tube or rod is rotated during manipulation

Glass-maker's soap A decolourising agent in the form of oxide of manganese or of a compound of arsenic or nickel

Ice glass A roughened frozen appearance produced by plunging the hot glass for a moment in cold water and then reheating it

Kit-Cat glass A graceful baluster wine glass resembling those in a picture by Kneller of members of the Kit-Cat Club

Latticino, Latticinio or Lattimo Venetian method of decorating glass with opaque white threads in interlacing patterns

Lead glass Glass-of-lead–also known as flint glass. The English late seventeenth-century contribution to glass technology

Lehr or Leer Glass needs to be toughened by annealing. The glass is placed in a heated chamber (lehr or leer) and gradually cooled

Lithyalin An almost opaque glass marbled in strong colours made and patented *frp,* 1828 by Friedrich Egermann in Bohemia

Marver The iron table on which the molten glass can be rolled into a cylindrical or globular mass

Milk-glass Opaque white glass

Mould Made first of clay or carved stone, more recently of metal. The glass bubble can be blown into it, and this led to such sophisticated devices as the mechanical blowing of bottles by machinery in metal moulds, a process perfected in America in the nineteenth century

Murrhine bowls Famous in Antiquity–perhaps imitations in glass of patterned semi-precious stones such as agate or chalcedony

Nipt diamond waies Late seventeenth-century description (Ravenscroft's price-list of 1677) of a form of decoration in which trailed threads were pincered into a network

Paraison Hot glass blown into a bubble at the end of the hollow of blowing iron. This bubble, still attached to the tube, can be pressed or rolled, elongated, cut with shears, manipulated by tongs or pincers

Passglas A similar beaker to the *Stangenglas* but encircled by spiral or horizontal threads dividing it into roughly equal parts. The guest was required to drink exactly down to one of these lines before passing on the glass to his neighbour

Pâte de verre Powdered glass fired in a mould, sometimes used for designs in low relief, sometimes recalling semi-precious stones

Pontil An iron rod to which the partly made vessel can be transferred

Pressed glass Process introduced in America in 1827. Molten glass is placed in a metal mould determining the vessel's shape and into this is thrust a plunger, which forces the glass upwards to fill the entire mould

Prunts English term for the impressed pattern of raised dots (raspberry prunts) on the stems of the characteristic German *Roemer*–seventeenth century or later

Rock crystal Natural quartz which glassmen tried to imitate – and often improved upon

Schwarzlot Painting in black with slight touches of red and gold

Seeds Undissolved particles and bubbles of gas in imperfectly fused glass

Silesian stem A ribbed and high-shouldered wine glass stem of German origin fashionable for a time after the Treaty of Utrecht (1713) and the accession of George I the following year

Stangenglas (pole glass) Tall German beaker

Stipple engraving Making a design with a series of dots

Trailing Softened glass drawn out into threads, attached to a vessel and melted into it

Wheel engraving using a wheel worked by a treadle to make a design

Zwischengoldgläser Glasses in which a design on gold leaf was applied to the outside and an outer glass, fitting exactly, placed over it

Bought of John Burroughs at the Glasse house without Ludgate London.

100 Trade card of John Burroughs whose 'Glasse house without Ludgate' may have been that referred to in Pepys's diary for 23rd February 1669. Burroughs was Master of the Glass Sellers' Company in 1681-2. The engraving shows a furnace in an elaborate classical frame, with the proprietor facing us and the 'gaffer' seated in his chair with his 'pontil' on the arm and a gathering of molten glass at the end. Late seventeenth century.

Bibliography

Anyone who wishes to probe further into the history of glass will find himself confronted by a bewildering array of books, catalogues and articles in specialist magazines. The author ventures to make a selction as follows:-

Barrington Haynes, E. *Glass Through the Ages*. London, 1966.
Bickerton, L. M. *Eighteenth Century English Drinking Glasses*. London, 1971.
British Museum *Masterpieces of Glass*. London, 1968.
Buckley, Wilfred *The Art of Glass*. London, 1939.
Crompton, Sidney (ed.) *English Glass*. London, 1967.
Davis, Derek C. *English and Irish Antique Glass*. London, 1964.
Davis, Frank *The Country Life Book of Glass*. London, 1966.
Davis, Frank *Continental Glass. From Roman to Modern Times*. London, 1972.
Davis, Frank *Early 18th-century English Glass*. London, 1971.
Elville, E. M. *The Collector's Dictionary of Glass*. London, 1967.
Elville, E. M. *English Table Glass*. London, 1960.
Elville, E. M. *English and Irish Cut Glass*. London, 1964.
Frothingham, Alice *Spanish Glass*. London, 1964.
Gros-Galliner, Gabriella *Glass*. London, 1970.
Hartshorne, A. *Old English Glasses*. London, 1897.
Honey, W. B. *Glass. A Handbook and a Guide to the Museum Collection*. Victoria and Albert Museum, London, 1946
Hudig, Ferrand *Dutch Glass Engravers*. Privately printed, 1926.
Mariacher, Giovanni *Italian Blown Glass*. London, 1961
Neuberg, Frederic *Glass in Antiquity*. (Translated by R. J. Charleston). Havant, 1949.
Polak, Ada *Modern Glass*. London 1962.
Wakefield, Hugh *Nineteenth Century British Glass*. London, 1961

Acknowledgements

Photographs:
British Museum, London 5, 6, 7, 14, 15, 17, 18, 33, 35; British Publishing Corporation 82; Christie Manson and Woods, London 32, 53, 78, 96, 97, 98; Hamlyn Group – Hawkley Studio Associates 1, 2, 12, 21, 28, 31, 36, 41, 74, 75, 79, 81, 83, 84, endpapers; Hamlyn Group Picture Library 43, 44, 45, 50, 54, 69, 73, 100; Mallett at Bourdon House Ltd., London 63; Metropolitan Museum of Art, New York 46, 47, 49, 51, 52, jacket; Musée des Arts Décoratifs, Paris 62, 65; Museum für Kunst und Gewerbe, Hamburg 24, 30; National Portrait Gallery, London 23; Orrefors Glasbruk, Orrefors 72, 76, 77; Rheinisches Bildarchiv, Cologne 27; Scala, Florence 3; Sotheby and Company, London 34, 38, 42, 67, 70, 71, 88, 89, 90, 91, 92, 93, 94, 95, 99; Victoria and Albert Museum, London 4, 8, 9, 10, 11, 13, 16, 19, 20, 22, 25, 26, 29, 37, 39, 40, 55, 56, 57, 58, 59, 60, 61, 64 66, 68, 80, 85, 86, 87; Yale University Art Gallery, New Haven, Connecticut 48.

Index

Numbers in bold type refer to illustrations